GIFTED

GIFTED

How God Is Glorified

Jerry McDermott

iUniverse, Inc.
Bloomington

Gifted
How God Is Glorified

iUniverse books may be ordered through booksellers or by contacting:

iUniverse
1663 Liberty Drive
Bloomington, IN 47403
www.iuniverse.com
1-800-Authors (1-800-288-4677)

Because of the dynamic nature of the Internet, any web addresses or links contained in this book may have changed since publication and may no longer be valid. The views expressed in this work are solely those of the author and do not necessarily reflect the views of the publisher, and the publisher hereby disclaims any responsibility for them.

Any people depicted in stock imagery provided by Thinkstock are models, and such images are being used for illustrative purposes only.
Certain stock imagery © Thinkstock.

ISBN: 978-1-4759-5781-5 (sc)
ISBN: 978-1-4759-5782-2 (ebk)

Library of Congress Control Number: 2012919924

Printed in the United States of America

iUniverse rev. date: 10/27/2012

CONTENTS

PART 3
THE GIFTED

PART 4
EVER WONDER WHAT GOD THINKS?

PART 5
Appendix

"The fact is that whether you eat or drink-whatever you do-you should do all for the glory of God" (1 Corinthians 10:31).

Endorsements of the author's *A Gilded Walk—The Path to Heaven: 2010*

"Once destined for the priesthood, McDermott became instead a staff engineer at GTE and an account executive at Texas Instruments and eventually a lay pastor. He gives an account of his many rewarding spiritual experiences and his trust in God."
-Review by J.C. Martin in Arizona Daily Star-August, 2011

"Your book has helped my missionary efforts."
-Ralph Rogawski, O.P. 2011

"Glad to see your new book. Keep writing. You have a lot to give and there is a crowd waiting to hear the Good News. I think your writing is a charism that the Lord will use for his glory."
-Robert DeGrandis, S.S.J 2010

"A Gilded Walk is a highly inspirational book that explains, in depth, the importance of incorporating the Kingdom of God into our daily lives, here and now, while we are on earth, and the incredible peace and happiness that we can experience by inviting the Holy Spirit into our hearts, inspiring us to become more Christ-like.

The journey begins when we are baptized into God's family and continues as God guides us through the trials and tribulations throughout our lives and, ultimately, as He leads us into eternity. Along this journey, we have many opportunities to draw ourselves into an 'intimate relationship' with God which are clearly defined in this book. There are also many fascinating personal stories of the numerous ways God's power has worked in the author's life."

Reader's five star review **of** *A Gilded Walk,* Kindle Edition, at Amazon.com.-used with permission-2010

ACKNOWLEDGEMENTS

I owe much to Fr. Robert De Grandis, who was like a mentor to me with his Spirit-filled writings and conference teachings. My thanks, also, to Myles Munroe who introduced Kingdom Living via his writings. I'm also indebted to charismatic co-leaders and friends such as the Baiers, the Modes, the O'Reillys, and the Sankos. A special thank you to Mary, my wife, who was my reader, advisor, patient companion, and prayer partner. Thanks also go to my daughter, Erin, who again assisted me as a consultant. A special thanks goes to Colleen Aitken for her editing and Pastor Rick Leis for his encouragement and spiritual assistance.

PREFACE

The phrase, "You only go around once" seems to be the not-so latent modern philosophy. However, this seemingly simple expression has two results and they are both eternal. One is for secular living and the other is for spiritual living. Expanding on this, one choice abandons God's commandments while the other strives to obey God's directions. The choices we make daily determine our eternal positioning, heaven or hell.

I'd like to summarize the choices I made for my journey. Surprisingly, the only schools I ever attended were parochial schools and that included graduate school. It started with graduation from high school where I won honors in religion, a complete surprise. I continued my education at St. Mary's University where I won a major letter in journalism. I then joined a seminary. After graduating from the Pontifical Institute of Philosophy with a BA, I did graduate work at DePaul and bible studies at Franciscan University. During this time, I joined the work force and enlisted in the Air Force Reserve. However, during this era, I was probably straddling the secular and spiritual world.

In spite of the seminary experience, the changing point in my life to really get serious about God was the introduction of the Detroit Catholic Charismatic Renewal. Through a weekly seminar, I learned about the gifts that Jesus has for us to help build his kingdom and to improve our relationship with him as well as with others. Once I embraced the renewal, I stepped into the spiritual side. There were side excursions but Jesus forgave me and I was back on the journey. I was active in church parish affairs including the presidency of the parish council. Under the guidance of the Holy Spirit I became active in charismatic prayer groups and became a co-pastor of a group for years. I am now semi-retired and thankful that the Lord keeps his gifts dormant but ready. We will discuss these heavenly gifts in a few chapters so I don't want to steal my thunder now.

It is amazing that while the Holy Trinity of Father, Son, and Spirit were complete in themselves, they chose to share their love. While this is a great mystery, scripture tells us that God Is Love. Since love is a quality of sharing, this may explain God's incredible action in creating us with an eternal spirit. We are unlike plants and animals, not only with our intelligence, but also in our destiny to be with him forever. He has given believers numerous gifts for personal spiritual development as well extending his kingdom. Through centuries he has also spoken to us in many ways. He also gave us free will. Where we spend eternal life is up to us, depending how we respond to his gifts. Eternity doesn't have its ups and downs, but only one direction depending on our final judgment.

Why should we practice goodness in our lives to influence this judgment? The reason is mentioned many times in the book of Leviticus as "Be holy, for I the Lord, your God, am holy" (Leviticus 19.1). Jesus expressed the same mandate as, "In a word, you must be made perfect as your heavenly Father is perfect" (Matthew 5:48).

Both Peter and John expand this instruction further: "His divine power has given us everything we need for this life and godliness through our knowledge of great and precious promises so that through them you may participate in the divine nature and escape the corruption in the world caused by evil desires" (2 Peter 1:3-4 NIV). "Everyone who acts in holiness has been begotten by him" (1 John

2:29). He further astounds us with the teaching, "God is love and he who abides in love, abides in God and God in him" (1 John 4:16).

In *Gifted,* we will show the many spiritual tools God has made available to us to assist our growth in holiness. In addition, we have provided many years of his modern prophetic words that guided his followers.

Paul says he doesn't want us to be ignorant of spiritual gifts and we don't either. Therefore, we'll discuss the various ones listed in scripture plus the ones people are experiencing today including my own personal experiences.

Since the gift of prophecy is preferred by Paul, we have a special section covering about 35 years of modern prophetic words from prayer groups and churches.

Introduction

It seems there are five possible lives we can experience: our Physical Birth, our Christian Birth, Kingdom Living, Spirit-filled Living, and Eternal Life. Of course, not everyone experiences all these lives after birth. In fact, many only experience live birth and eternity. Yes, everyone is alive after birth. It's not something we choose, but an action our parents chose. Now being born again into the Christian life is our choice and what a wonderful decision as it influences an eternal life with God.

Part of being born again is water baptism, which is a further declaration of intent. However, in some mainline churches, infants are water-baptized into the church. The question is whether as an adult they re-affirm the parental decision for them when they were a baby?

I suddenly realized the status of modern adulthood when starting to read the Book of Proverbs. It happened in Chapter 1, Verse 7 which reads, "The fear of the Lord is the beginning of knowledge, wisdom, and instruction (that) fools despise."

Time out while we mention that this word, fear, is not being afraid nor is it being a scared-y-cat. Scriptural fear implies a respect or holding someone or something in awe. "Thus all who dwell on the earth shall know, and all who inhabit the world shall understand that nothing is better than the fear of the Lord, nothing more salutary than to obey his commandments" (Sirach 23:27). This explanation should give you a clue of the modern problem. I believe we have become the Lost and Found generation.

What we have lost is the respect for God's kingship, goodness, and sovereignty. Our culture does not have latent disrespect for Jesus Christ but open disregard for his sacrifice. Imagine that the creator provided a means whereby sinful mankind would be returned to relationship with God. Jesus further emphasized that without contrition and belief in him, mankind cannot achieve a heavenly eternity.

Since some people rejected God's plan, what did they find on their own? The answer is unbridled hedonism, the self-indulgence in every aspect of modern life. As an example, immorality suddenly became the norm in the entertainment industry. With instant news, our sinful nature is portrayed on the nightly news yet there isn't any judgment of wrong doing. That would be politically incorrect being against individual freedoms.

We have lost respect for honestly, morality, modesty, marriage and family life. We have removed God from our schools even though our nation was dedicated to God by our founders. We could go on and on about our degradation as a nation. Instead, let's move to examine the good life available to those who align themselves with God's system.

The subtitle of *Gifted* mentions that God is glorified. The question is, "But how?" The answer is contained in the prayer of Jesus to the Father: "I have given you the glory on earth by finishing the work you gave me to do" (John 17:4). Earlier, John tells us Jesus manifested his glory for the first time at the Cana wedding feast. (John 2:11b).

What happened in the life of Jesus that suddenly his glory was revealed? The answer is that the Holy Spirit came upon him with the Baptism in the Jordan River. Later, Jesus said, "As the Father has sent me, so I send you" (John 20:21b). He also said that the Father would give the disciples another Paraclete or intercessor to be with them always. Therefore, as we receive the Holy Spirit, this is how we imitate Jesus and give glory to the Father. Jesus said, "My Father has been glorified in your bearing much fruit and becoming my disciples." We are the modern Spirit-filled disciples. For this reason Paul speaks to us, "Everything written before our time was written for our instruction" (Romans 15:4a).

While this is titled, *Gifted,* we have to remember the words of Jesus when he said that we did not choose him, he chose us. The gifts are his via the Holy Spirit.

All gifts can be considered greater or lesser such as gold and silver versus cloth or clay. The same is true in the biblical sense. However, scripture teaches us that all gifts come from God, but two gifts are beyond qualification.

The gift of salvation is classical in that while it is available to all, it is not active until it is sought and received. This is the reality of John 3:16 that we see proclaimed in public or sports events. It is the reality Jesus spoke about as being born again. The reception of this gift is the spiritual birth into the kingdom of God. The procedure is accepting Jesus as Lord and Savior and asking forgiveness of our sins.

While the gift of salvation grants eternal life with our loving God, there is a further blessing for this life. This is the infilling of the Holy Spirit.

Jesus said we would also do his works and commanded us to go forth. How could we possibly imitate him? We certainly could not become divine! The secret is that he became fully man like us. He said we would receive power when the Holy Spirit came upon us. This repeats *his* baptism in the Jordan when the Holy Spirit came upon him and he began his ministry. This same anointing can be ours by asking for the Baptism of the Holy Spirit. The result is the gifts outlined in the next chapters. Like salvation, these gifts are available, but not received until they are sought and accepted. Jesus taught us, "If you, with all your sins, know how to give your children what is good, how much more will your heavenly Father give good things to anyone who asks" (Matthew 7:11).

Of course, everyone loves a gift. After all, our favorites are birthday and holiday surprises. We look forward to receiving them as well as giving them. Also there can be a myriad of little gifts throughout the year. While most personal gifts are usually surprises, numerous spiritual gifts are mentioned in scripture.

Therefore, we will investigate many spiritual gifts. However, the main emphasis must be that these gifts come from God to build his kingdom. St. Paul summarizes gifts so well by stating, "Name something you have that you have not received. If then, you have received it, why are you boasting as if it were your own" (1 Cor. 4:7)?

The corollary to this is that a gift is not a gift until it is received. That is the problem with spiritual gifts as they are generally unclaimed. Paul tells us to seek the spiritual gifts (1 Corinthians 14:1b). Attending church is wonderful and quite necessary for growth. Paul is telling us that here is something beyond the Sunday service. The power inherent in the spiritual gifts is for kingdom as well as personal growth.

Speaking of the power of the Holy Spirit, Jesus clarified this so well by stating that the world at large cannot receive him because it is not looking for him and doesn't recognize him. I did recognize him and much of the book stems from conversations with God that I entered in journals so I would not forget God's words. Christianity is a personal relationship with God with each party communicating with the other. Having a conversation is the best word to describe this wonderful relationship with our creator. Scripture shows this in the Garden of Eden when God walked and talked with Adam and Eve.

PART 1
THE GIFT

CHAPTER 1

LIFE

Nothingness. Have you ever thought about it? Have you ever tried to describe nothingness? You can say that nothing existed at one time, but that isn't true. The reality is that nothing that was created existed. The certainty is that God existed, but there wasn't anything else. There wasn't anything to see, nor to hear because there wasn't anything around. The modern thought that everything came from nothing is strange since there is no recognition of a creator. How can nothing come together with nothing else to produce something unless it is by God as the creator?

One day that started to change as the sky and the earth were created and were revealed when God created light. As the days progressed, God continued with all the preparations for his masterpiece. First, he created living things as plants and animals.

Then, he created man in his image. Since God is a Spirit, it is this part in us that is godlike, not our physical appearance. This fact is staggering that the creator of the universe wanted to share his life with us. He did not choose plants or animals as he didn't equip them with eternal life, or an immortal soul. His purpose was to have a relationship with mankind. He proved this in the Book of Genesis when it tells of God walking and talking with Adam and Eve.

The creator who is Love wants to share that love with each of us. We were destined to have a personal relationship with God, our creator. Until you understand this, you will not realize that any religion or denominational differences are a collection of rules, devotions, rituals, and procedures rather than a personal relationship with God.

CHAPTER 2

ANOTHER LIFE

Unfortunately, our ancestor's negated God's command. The byproduct was a lifelong separation from God. His original intention was thwarted by his creature. Man was still alive, but was now spiritually dead. We could not achieve the personal relationship with God without forgiveness of our corporate sin.

Have you ever wondered why we are held accountable for something that happened thousands of years ago? Why should that sin affect us? The answer is rather simple, but was unknown fully until recent years. It is that we bear the DNA of Adam and Eve just as every human being. Their disobedience created a chasm between God and man not just in this life, but eternally. Later, we'll discuss God's plan, known to him before He even created man. For the present, we'll look at various religions man has invented to solve the gap between God and man. All the journeys postulate a path to God. They reason that since God is loving, He would not cause anyone to suffer. Even some Christians believe these false ideas.

I call them erroneous attempts at eternal life for one reason: they reject God's plan, the creator's incredible sacrifice. The refusal of God's plan and the substitution of man's reasoning leads to a fiery eternal life. Physical death does not mean absolute death as we were created in God's spirit image wherein life is eternal.

Let's review. God created us to be with him forever and gave us a scriptural guide, the bible, and commandments that would ensure our happiness and life with Him. Man had a better idea and we all suffer as a result and are ordained for a hellish future life unless we follow the creator's redemption plan. Everyone attending a sports event has seen the sign, **John 3:16**. Remember, God created us even knowing that our forefathers would turn against him. For that reason, he sacrificed his only son that we could be redeemed and re-establish that personal relationship with him. The scripture for John 3:16 reveals that, "God so loved the world that he gave his only son that whoever believes in him may not die, but have eternal life." This explanation continues: "Whomever believes in him avoids condemnation; but whoever does not believe is already condemned for not believing in the name of God's only Son. The judgment of condemnation is this: "The light came into the world, but men loved darkness rather than light because their deeds were wicked" (John 3:18-19). Simply expressed, our choice is eternal bliss with God or doing our thing, which results in a fiery separation from all that is good.

At Christmas each year, we celebrate the birth of Jesus Christ. The impact of this birth is that the Son of God grew up and died for us. Rising from the dead, he became our redeemer and restored the relationship with God.

Let us examine why anyone would knowingly choose what is a false hope. The modern approach to heaven is that there is one God and all roads lead to him. This sounds good at first glance, but is based on human reasoning not divine plans. In *A Gilded Walk*, I showed that when you arrive in heaven, there is a door. The only way that heavenly door will open is an existing belief in Jesus Christ as Savior. Jesus confirmed this by saying, "I am the way, and the truth, and the life; no one comes to the Father but through me" (John 14:6).

Some people claim a future residence in heaven based on their estimation of living an earthly good life. Jesus anticipated this faulty belief by stating, "None of those who cry out, 'Lord, Lord,' will enter the kingdom of God, but only the one who does the will of my Father in heaven. Then I will declare to them solemnly, I never knew you" (Matthew 7:21-23). If we did not make any effort to accept Jesus in this life, why should he accept us in the next life? As I showed in *A Gilded Walk,* religion is not conforming to a set of rules, but a real relationship with God, a personal relationship. Without a relationship with God now, there is no relationship in a future life and certainly a dwelling devoid of goodness.

People wonder that since we all worship the same God, what's the problem? The problem is that without believing in Jesus Christ and his atonement for our sins as the Son of God, you are not worshipping the one true God and our sinful nature is still there. Scripture clearly states what our nature is without remission. God has fortunately guided and assisted us in living a life acceptable to him by listing some no-no's. These are commonly called the commandments.

There were many *shalt nots* in the Old Testament that regulated life, worship, and morals. In the New Testament, the *shalt nots* refer to sin or immorality that separate us from God. But ordinary living is not structurally regimented. However, so many Christians continue to see religion as something rigid. It seems that many of the mainline churches have such rigid rules which follow from their interpretation of a scripture passage.

God clarified this new life to Peter with a vision of all the animals of earth. The sacrifice of Jesus had replaced the requirements of the old law. The angel expanded this by saying, "What God has purified, you are not to call unclean". Paul understood through his experience that some would focus on man-made rules and not a relationship with God. He summarized the teaching given him to the Colossians, "No one is free therefore to pass judgment on you in terms of what you eat or drink or what you do on yearly or monthly feasts or on the Sabbath" (Colosians2:16-17). He then asked that since they have died to cosmic forces with Christ, why should they be bound by rules such as, "Do not handle! Do not taste! Do not touch! As though they were still living a life bounded by this world? Such prescriptions dealt with things that perished in their use. They were based on merely human precepts and doctrines. While these make a certain show of wisdom in their affected piety, humility, and bodily austerity, their chief affect is that they indulge men's pride" (Colossians 2:20-23.

Frequently, you will come across someone who is against some form of food or drink. Instead of debating the subject, Paul gave us wisdom in such circumstances: "Let your speech be always gracious and in good taste, and strive to respond properly to all who address you" (Colossians 4:6). There is nothing wrong with fasting or refraining from something for prayerful means as long as the connection to God's word is mindful. In that regard, we are mindful of Paul's words to Timothy, "Take a little wine for the good of your stomach" (1 Timothy 5:23).

CHAPTER 3

KINGDOM LIVING

For many people, the idea of living in a kingdom is foreign to their experience. We are very familiar with the British royalty which are historic figureheads, but loved by their people. In addition, we are familiar with the faults of so many historical kings that we have trouble imaging a different kind of kingdom ruled by a benevolent king. Living in a spiritual kingdom is nothing like an earthly kingdom. The kingdom of God is ruled by the Son of God and therefore not subject to the vagaries or whims of a human king.

For years, people have prayed the Our Father which states that the kingdom of God will happen on earth as it is already established in heaven. But before discussing the earthly kingdom, we will examine what it isn't in order to cancel any pre-notions. "The kingdom of God is not a matter of eating or drinking, but a matter of justice, peace and the joy of the Holy Spirit" (Romans 14:17).

Why is food mentioned? We refer to the sixth chapter of Matthew where it states that our heavenly Father takes care of such important needs. A modern expression, "Why Worry?" seems to capture the meaning. The other attributes of such living is the result where God is the head. In addition, Jesus taught that we don't live only by bread, but by every word that comes from the mouth of God, in other words, the bible.

Searching scripture, you will find the kingdom is the main topic of preaching and teaching in the New Testament. By contrast, the church is only mentioned a few times. John the Baptist was the last prophet living in the old covenant to proclaim that the reign of God was at hand. (Matthew 3:26). When Jesus started his public ministry he started to proclaim, "Reform your lives! The kingdom of heaven is at hand" (Matthew 4:17).

This teaching, or command, was previewed in the Old Testament. "As your reward for heeding these decrees (or commandments), and observing them carefully, the Lord, your God, will keep with you the merciful covenant which he promised on oath to your fathers. He will love, bless and multiply you; he will bless the fruit of your womb and the produce of your soil, your grain and wine and oil, the issue of your herds and the young of your flocks in the land which he swore to your fathers he would give you. You will be blessed above all peoples; no man or woman among you shall be childless nor shall your livestock be barren. The Lord will remove all sickness from you" (Deuteronomy 7:12-15a).

In the New Testament, Jesus said, "I warn you, then, do not worry about your livelihood, what you are to eat or drink or use for clothing. Is not life more than food? Is not the body more valuable than clothes? Stop worrying then, over questions like, what are we to eat or what are we to drink, or what are we to wear? The unbelievers are always running after these things. Your heavenly Father knows all that you need. Seek first his kingship over you, his way of holiness and all these things will be given you besides" (Matthew 6:25, 31-33). Note the fact that when we live in God's kingdom we have a holy king over us that will look after us in all things.

CHAPTER 4

A SANCTIFIED LIFE

I like the way that small words in scripture can have such a major impact. See if you can spot such a word in this narrative: "Jesus performed this first of his signs at Cana in Galilee" (John 2:11). The word is *first.* If this was the initial miracle in the life of Jesus, how did his life suddenly change? What happened that people in the synagogue asked each other, "Where did this man get such wisdom and miraculous powers" (Matthew 13:54b)?

Some would say that he could always work miracles, but it just wasn't his time until Cana. Others might say, "Well, he was God wasn't he?" Both explanations miss the point that Jesus put his Godhead aside to be fully human (Philippians 2:6). Paul repeated Psalm 8 which said, "You have made him little less than the angels" (Hebrews 2:7). What happened was that Jesus was filled with the Holy Spirit after the baptism by John the Baptist. If Jesus had retained his full Trinitarian deity, how could he receive the Holy Spirit if he already had the Holy Spirit? Peter emphasizes this point in the Cornelius discourse. He said God had anointed Jesus with the Holy Spirit and power. Jesus then performed good works and healing. The point is that Jesus had such great love that he humbled himself to become like us.

After being Spirit-filled, Jesus began his ministry. Jesus had previously told the apostles that they would receive power when the

Holy Spirit came down upon them fulfilling his Father's promise (Acts 1:7-9). Interestingly, this was the last instruction Jesus gave them before his Ascension into heaven. The apostles and disciples were to be his representatives and spread the good news and perform the same acts as Jesus, including miracles.

Some will negate the call for all people in all ages to share the good news of this new life. They say that this was just for the apostolic age, not today. Scripture says otherwise in at least two places. The first says that, "Everything written before our time was written for our instruction, that we might derive hope from the lesson of patience and the words of encouragement in the scriptures" (Romans 15:4). In the Book of Acts, Peter states that the Holy Spirit was promised to the people he was addressing and their children as well as those far off for whom the Lord calls (Acts 2:39). Interestingly, the last word in Peter's Pentecostal talk was a prophecy for all generations: "Save yourself from this generation which has gone astray" (Acts 2:40b). This is certainly a prophetic truth for the modern era in which we live

For some folks, religion is going to church on Sunday, maybe experiencing a few fervent moments in their lifetime and passing away. This certainly is not the life that Jesus led, or the life he promised those who followed Him. Reflecting on the words of Jesus before Pentecost, Paul clearly understood this message by stating, "Be filled with the Spirit" (Ephesians 5:18b).

This is also our heritage. Paul enumerated the Gifts of the Holy Spirit and said he didn't want the Corinthians (and everyone else) to be ignorant of spiritual gifts. (1 Corinthians 12:1). Never one to mince words, Paul also told the people from Corinth, "Some of you are quite ignorant of God" (1 Corinthians 15:34a).

While we receive the Holy Spirit by being born again, it is with the Baptism of the Holy Spirit that these gifts are released for service within the kingdom. This is the usual method whereby we grow to the full maturity of Christ and no longer search out every false doctrine being proclaimed (Ephesians 4:15). Why is there still widespread ignorance of God's desire for his power within us? I called this chapter a holy or sanctified life as that life is available to all Christians. It is the true imitation of Christ that the apostles experienced. Imagine the change in mindset among these Jewish followers of Jesus. In Exodus 19, God told Moses that the people were not to climb Mt. Sinai or to even touch its base. Verse 19 says that if they touched the mountain when Moses and the Lord were together, they were to be killed In other words, stay clear as only God and Moses were to be so close. Now the same Holy Spirit that came upon Jesus was to fall upon his close followers at Pentecost and for each of us as believers. Jesus lives in us by the Holy Spirit.

There is a wonderful example of this gift explained when Peter and John went to Samaria. Luke explains that they went there to pray that the people might receive the Holy Spirit (Acts 8:15). He continues that since they had *only* been baptized in the name of Jesus Christ, the Holy Spirit hadn't come down on them. Did you catch that word "only?" These folks were born again in having accepted Jesus as Lord and had received the Holy Spirit as a result. However, the power of the Holy Spirit had not been released in their lives. As a result, the gifts and fruit of the Holy Spirit were not operative in their everyday happenings and church meetings. The gifts were not operative for ministry, nor was the fruit of the Holy Spirit functioning to increase their holiness. It would seem minimalist to say that the same opportunity could be missing in our lives. This baptism is for the church's growth as well for our personal growth.

Chapter 5

ETERNAL LIFE

Are there multiple roads to heaven? Some people say, "There are so many gods, it's a difficult decision to follow which one, but I'm sure it does not matter which one you follow". Others say that if you are faithful to your own god and lead a good life, then everything will be okay. A corollary is that I don't go to church, but I'm a nice person and I help others so I know god will honor that. Another fervent belief is that god is not so demanding that you can only follow the Christian way. After all, "there are many roads to heaven." Yes, and each of those roads is a religion which has been formulated by man with rules to reach their god. These are all beautiful, heartwarming expressions of mankind. Unfortunately, they do not matter for it is only what God says that matters. As creator and sovereign Lord, thee one God has a different opinion and his inspired writings or scriptures say otherwise. Have you considered what God has said?

"I am the first and the last. There is no God but me" (Isaiah 44:6).

"All who make idols are nothing and the things they treasure are worthless" (Isaiah 44:9 (NIV).

"It was I who made the earth and created mankind upon it. It was my hands that stretched out the heavens" (Isaiah 45:12).

"Who announced this from the beginning and foretold it from old? Was it not I, the Lord, besides whom there is no other God. There is no just and saving God but me" (Isaiah 45:21-22).

If there were many ways to achieve heaven, God would not have sent his only begotten Son to suffer an ignominious death. Having established the validity of the one true God, his plan to redeem mankind was to send his Son who would be crucified and die for mankind, thus re-establishing the relationship between God and man. This is the primary reason Jesus could say, "I am the Way, the Truth and the Life." Non-Christian religions do not accept God's way: the sacrifice of his Son. Scripture repeatedly speaks to the people about living the new way or the redeemed way of life in Christ. But Paul also tells the Romans that some people instinctively kept the law without knowledge of it (Romans 2:14-16). This is the purpose of life that God has placed in everyone.

This was demonstrated after Pentecost when the gathered throngs of people heard Peter's inspired talk. They cried out asking what they should do. Peter replied, "You must reform and be baptized, each one of you in the name of Jesus Christ, that your sins may be forgiven; then you will receive the gift of the Holy Spirit" (Acts 2:37-39).

The roads to God are one of judgment and not salvation unless you are born again in which case the promise of heaven is already experienced. There isn't a variety of ways to salvation. They are all dead ends except for God's way, salvation through his Son. Imagine the creator, the everlasting God, so loved his creation that turned against him, that he assigned his only Son to suffer and die such a death. By this action mankind would be redeemed if they accepted his Son. Looked at this way, it is difficult to favor God's wrath rather than his love. Either way, eternity is involved, happiness or condemnation.

It is difficult to get a handle on eternity, which is timeless. Today, time is our constant companion due to schedules, appointments, family duties, and favorite TV shows. Considering this dichotomy, I once asked the Lord about this. He replied, "What is forever? It is a moment with me that never ceases. You already know how to praise me, how to love me and accept my love. But forever began when you accepted me. It never stops yet seems like only a minute for we share such oneness. I long for you as you long for me yet we are one in spite of such longing and desire. Now I will tell you something—there is so much more of my infinite love that you cannot imagine. You think you know love now; I tell you it has just begun for I have so many things planned for my people. You will be amazed at the depth of my love for those who up to now aren't even aware of my love. Help me build the kingdom to join you as friends and fellow believers. I will help you. Fear not."

Only our Lord could phrase such wonders. Notice how He changed the concept of time being the past, the present and the future into eternity. He also explained John's proclamation that "We have come to know and believe in the love God has for us. God is love and he who abides in love abides in God and God in him" (1 John 4:16). I always wondered how we could live in God. The answer is through love. The reply about forever is the most beautiful word the Lord has ever spoken other than, **"I love you."**

Where and what is this place where believers will spend eternal life? The place is generally called heaven or paradise and is the dwelling place of almighty God. It is described as the new Jerusalem, a city of immense size and beauty ornate with precious stones and gold (Revelation 21:18-19).

Paul gives us a preview by repeating an earlier passage (Isaiah 64:3): "Eye has not seen; ear has not heard, nor has it so much as dawned on man what God has prepared for those who love him" (1 Corinthians 2:9). This is not a mythical description but something that has form and structure, something that can be appreciated by our God-given senses.

Jesus anticipated our quandary about eternity in a wonderful passage in John's gospel. Jesus looked to heaven and said, "Father, the hour has come! Give glory to your Son that your Son may give glory to you, inasmuch as you have given him authority over all mankind that he may bestow eternal life on those you gave him. Eternal life is this: to know you, the only true God and him who you sent, Jesus Christ" (John 17:1-2).

While I am typing this, 2012 is an election year. I pray that all American citizens will get out and vote. Christians have a dual citizenship, that of their country and the heavenly kingdom. When saying the Our Father, have you ever considered that you are agreeing that God's kingdom will occur because it is his will? That kingdom starts here and is fulfilled in us when we reach heaven. That is why Christians should have no fear of dying. It is only a transition from an earthly life with Christ to a heavenly life with Christ and his glory. Some fear punishment for sins even though they have already been forgiven. John recognized this and under the anointing wrote that our love is not perfected if we have any notion of fear and punishment in the next life

There is another aspect of eternal life and that is reserved to those who reject the Son of God and the Father's plan for salvation. The place is commonly called hell and has numerous scriptural references. So many words refer to the life there, but most people have heard of suffering, damnation and hell fire. There is a sense of being in a vacuum as there is a complete absence of the love of God.

PART 2
THE GIFTS

CHAPTER 6

INTRODUCTION TO SPIRITUAL GIFTS

Many people equate religion with a lot of preaching in tents or churches. Paul said otherwise. "The kingdom of God does not consist in talk, but in power" (1 Corinthians 4:20). Jesus promised this same power when he said, "You will receive power when the Holy Spirit comes down on you" (Acts 1:8a). He was speaking to his followers about the action of the Holy Spirit on the Jewish feast of Pentecost. This same power released by spiritual gifts is available to every follower of Christ. Consider that Jesus said that we would do the works he did (John 14:12).

In spite of numerous references in scripture, most people do not have knowledge of the spiritual gifts as they usually aren't taught in seminaries or in non-charismatic churches. Therefore, if you do not know about the gifts, or charisms, we have listed them according to usage in various scriptures. When the Holy Spirit anoints you and you use one of these gifts, you will understand something completely new. Jesus said, "It was not you who chose me, it was I who chose you" (John 15:16a). Besides, using the God-given gifts gives God the glory. The practice of religion is more than a church service. Let us take a look at these scriptural gifts before we examine them in detail.

SUMMARY IN SCRIPTURE

1 Corinthians 12:6-11
Wisdom, knowledge, faith, healing, miracles, prophecy, discernment, tongues, and interpretation

Romans 12:6-8
Prophecy, ministry, teacher, exhortation, alms giving, mercy works, ruler

Ephesians 4:11
Apostles, prophets, evangelists, pastors, teachers

Summary By Type
Word Gifts—tongues, interpretation, prophecy
Intellectual Gifts—discernment, wisdom, knowledge
Power Gifts—healing, miracles, faith

Summary By Service
Charismatic Gifts—1 Corinthians 12:4-11
Ministerial Gifts—Ephesians 4:11, 1 Corinthians 12:28-30
Motive Gifts—Romans 12:6-8; 1 Peter 4: 10-11

COMMENT

Seven gifts are listed in Isaiah 11:1 as: wisdom; understanding; counsel; fortitude; knowledge; piety; and fear of the Lord. These gifts listed in the Old Testament are stated as permanent dispositions. Paul shows that while the nine gifts are given by the Spirit, in particular anointings, there are also ministerial gifts. He lists these as prophecy; ministry; teaching; exhortation; alms giving; leadership; and works of mercy. (Romans 12:6-8).

CHAPTER 7

TONGUES

THE SUPERNATURAL LANGUAGE

I grew up in an era where I drove my mother crazy as we waited for the mail carrier to bring the latest secret decoder ring. Things have not changed much today with user names and passwords for everything. God foresaw code words long ago. Have you ever thought that the gift of tongues is a twofold gift? It really is the code to the language of the Trinity. It is also a secret language giving us the ability to communicate with God, absolutely protected from any satanic understanding or interference.

What a wonderful gift as the Holy Spirit prays to the Father or Jesus through us. Many times, we just don't know what to say in prayer. Paul realized this and explained, "The Spirit too helps us in our weaknesses, for we do not know how to pray as we ought; but the Spirit himself makes intercession for us with groaning that cannot be expressed in speech. He who searches hearts knows what the Spirit means, for the Spirit intercedes for the saints as God himself wills" (Romans 8:26-27).

I know numerous people who have the gift of tongues, but do not use the gift. Tongues are great to start morning prayers or whenever you are driving. Paul is quite firm about using the gift saying, "At every opportunity pray in the Spirit" (Ephesians 6:18a). He also says, "Do not stifle the Spirit" (1 Thessalonians 5:19a).

Remember the last time you said the Our Father? How many times were you interrupted? I know I never get far before my mind wanders off into something supposedly important as daily tasks. With tongues you can speak to God with your mind on something else, hopefully spiritual. When you want to know what you are praying about, just ask the Holy Spirit.

When you are initially baptized in the Holy Spirit, you will usually be given a prayer language which may change in time. Then you will have multiple private languages. In addition, the Spirit may give you a one-time language for special situations.

One day, I was praying with someone over the phone and they had to hang up as they were expecting another call. I left my office and went into the living room and continued to pray for the person. The Lord said that he had a word for them and I was to send an e-mail. This is the first time I had ever written in tongues. I thought about it and as the anointing came on me, I spelled each word phonetically in the e-mail. Of course, I introduced the subject in English. Several days later, I had to e-mail and ask the person that when they pronounced the words verbally, did they get the interpretation as I only got the words, not the meaning or interpretation. Their answer was, "Yes, I did and I did what was asked, too. Turned out to be lovely." Well, that was a first time for me. The Holy Spirit continues to surprise us and will use whatever means he wants.

Do you remember the narration in Acts where the Holy Spirit came upon the apostles and they spoke in tongues? Then the people understood them in their own language. (Acts 2:1-12) It seems this was a swift occurrence between the reception and the usage. The reality is that a great deal of time may have been involved.

Scripture says, "When the day of Pentecost came it found them gathered in one place." Most people assume this means a little after daybreak. Actually, the Jewish day begins at sundown on the day before. Therefore, the Holy Spirit may have come upon the folks in the upper room the day before they came outside and the gathered crowd heard them speak.

This sounds like a mystery, but is very simple. One of the first indications of the infilling of the Holy Spirit is the private prayer language or tongues. Probably, the people in the upper room spent the night praying ecstatically. The next morning they went outside and spoke in other tongue languages which the crowd heard in their own language. This sounds reasonable as it is unlikely that the crowd heard them praying in the upper room. Furthermore, the crowd identified them as Galileans and the only way they would know that was if the apostles and disciples were standing there.

One day I was speaking with a lady and I asked if she were baptized in the Holy Spirit. When she said, "Yes", I asked if she spoke in tongues. She floored me when she said, "Yes, I speak to my cat!" I could not help smiling and explained that tongues was something a little different. As she had already received the Baptism of the Holy Spirit, we prayed together and she received the gift of tongues.

CHAPTER 8

INTERPRETATION

UNDERSTANDING TONGUES

The best example of this is to examine the day of Pentecost when the newly Spirit-filled folks addressed the Jews gathered from many nations. Regardless of their backgrounds, they each heard the gospel in their native tongue. They were astounded. (Acts 2:6)

The most common usage of this gift is as a prophecy where under the anointing, someone will give a prophecy in tongues. Then the speaker or someone else will give the interpretation of what God wants to say.

I have experienced both of these examples plus a third one. In this case, I knew the person would be given the understanding not me. However, while prophesizing in tongues, I received a vision. After I finished, I usually waited while the person digested what they just heard and then told them the vision. Sometimes, this helped them understand the words or heightened the perception.

CHAPTER 9

PROPHECY

GOD SPEAKS HIS THOUGHTS THROUGH US

Among all the gifts, prophecy is the most favored. This thought sharply appears in the Old Testament: "Would that all the people of the Lord were prophetic. Would that the Lord might bestow his Spirit on them all" (Numbers 11:29). In the New Testament, Paul said, "Set your hearts on spiritual gifts-above all, the gift of prophecy" (1 Cor. 13:16). Peter explains that "Prophecy has never been put forward by man's willing it. It is rather that man impelled by the Holy Spirit have spoken under God's influence" (2 Peter 1:21). Furthermore, Paul said that the gift of prophecy is for encouragement and consolation (1 Corinthians 14:1-5). But, Paul also warns, "Do not despise prophecy" (1Thess. 5:20).

When the words "Thus saith The Lord" initially preceded the full prophetic expression in the Old Testament, they were like a thunderclap around the world. These are recognized as the first prophetic words that God wanted to be shared with all his chosen people. It was the Lord speaking through ordinary folks.

Perhaps a good question is why has he been speaking to us over the years? His original plan was that we were together so there wasn't any need. In the book of Genesis, a typical day was described where God walked and talked with Adam and Eve. However, the couple

25

had a better idea which disobeyed God's command. As a result, they lost the paradise God had created for them as well as for us. God created mankind wanting to share His love and longs for us to return. Therefore, throughout history he has communicated either in person or through his prophets.

Starting in Chapter 22, the book of Numbers has a wonderful explanation of prophecy. The elders of Moab and Midian came to Balaam asking for direction. Balaam answered, "Stay here overnight and I will give you whatever answer the Lord gives me" (Numbers 22:8).

God will not be silenced. As a result, there are at least two times where he surprises us. The passage in Numbers 22, verse 28 shows where he used a talking ass. With His triumphant entry into Jerusalem, the religious leaders told Jesus to stifle the disciples and the people. Jesus replied, "If they were to keep silence, I tell you the very stones would cry out" (Luke 19:40).

Back in Numbers, Balaam explained the plight of being a prophet in numerous verses:

— "What power have I to say anything? I can speak only what the Lord puts in my mouth" (Numbers 22:38).
— "Is it not what the Lord puts in my mouth that I must repeat with care" (Numbers 23:12)?
— "Did I not warn you that I must do all that the Lord tells me" (Numbers 23:26)?
— "I could not of my own accord do anything good or evil contrary to the command of the Lord. Whatever the Lord says, I must repeat" (Numbers 24:13).

One of the most beautiful biblical verses explains how Moses was a prophet. "Should there be a prophet among you, in visions will I reveal myself to him; in dreams will I speak to him; Not so with my servant Moses! Throughout my house, he bears my trust: face to face I speak to him, plainly and not in riddles. The presence of the Lord he beholds" (Numbers 12:6-8).

The early prophets spoke mainly of the coming Messiah to the Jewish people. Jesus fulfilled those prophecies and spoke many more prophecies to guide us. This is confirmed in scriptures which said, "In times past, God spoke in fragmentary and varied ways to our fathers through the prophets; in this final age, he has spoken to us through his Son whom he has made heir of all things and through whom he first created the universe" (Hebrews 1:1-2).

Since the church was formed at Pentecost, God has sent his Holy Spirit to dwell within us. The wonderful result is that each Spirit-filled Christian can function at times with the gift of prophecy as well as any of the other eight gifts of the Spirit. Paul talks about this wonderful gift in the 13th chapter of Corinthians. "Set your hearts on spiritual gifts, above all, the gift of prophecy" (1Cor. 13:1a). He also tells us that the prophet builds up, encourages, and consoles people. Comparing tongues as a personal prayer language with prophecy, he says that tongues build up the person while prophecy builds up the church. He also explains that a prophecy in tongues is also meaningful if it is interpreted. In this case, the church is edified. In addition, Peter warned us that, "First, you must understand this: there is no prophecy contained in scripture which is a personal interpretation. Prophecy has never been put forward by man's willing it. It is rather that men impelled by the Holy Spirit have spoken under God's influence" (2 Peter 1:20-21). This is an ageless truth but scripture warns that in the last days there will be false prophets to misguide the faithful. The modern prophets themselves must use discernment as well as the listener does.

2011 was an interesting year. With nature roaring and the economy vacillating, people were fearful of the future. However, even a cursory study of scriptures shows that God's constant mandate is to withstand the constant onslaught of fear. This comforting thought is proven by God's stating, "The Lord God does nothing without revealing his plan to his servants, the prophets" (Amos 3:7).

Here is a wonderful scriptural explanation of prophecy and the responsibilities of the prophet to speak God's words: "God is not man that he should speak falsely, nor human that he should change his mind. Is he one to speak and not act, to decree and not fulfill" (Numbers 23:19)?

CHAPTER 10

DISCERNMENT

SUPERNATURAL GUIDANCE OF RIGHT AND WRONG

Have you ever said, "Oh, that doesn't sound right?" That was discernment. If you had that thought during a sermon or a church conference, that may have been the gift of discernment. It could be either a natural thought based on experience or the supernatural gift. At one church we attended, one particular speaker usually caused me to elbow my wife. Something he said just did not sit right with me. When we got home, I would dive into the books and show my wife that scripture did not support his premise. However, discernment has a much wider application in our modern enlightenment than just evaluating sermons.

The Holy Spirit enlightened the bible writers with numerous examples. In fact, Peter wrote a warning for all generations: "In times past there were false prophets among God's people and among you also there will be false teachers who will smuggle in pernicious heresies. They will go so far as to deny the Master who acquired them for his own, thereby bringing on themselves swift disaster. Their lustful ways will lure many away. Through them, the true way will be made subject to contempt. They will deceive you with fabricated tales in a spirit of greed" (2 Peter 2:1-3).

Consider applying these precepts to New Age philosophy, cults, and other modern teachings. This also includes Christian denominations that have modified the gospel or changed it to Replacement Theology. The apostle John warns us to question every spirit and even tells us how to discern them: "Do not trust every spirit, but put the spirits to a test to see if they belong to God, because many false prophets have appeared in this world. This is how you can recognize God's Spirit: every spirit that acknowledges Jesus Christ came in the flesh belongs to God; while every spirit that fails to acknowledge him does not belong to God." (1 John 4:1-3).

There are actually three spirits to checkout: a heavenly spirit, an evil spirit, and us. Yes, the latter one can be our spirit or ego. Some writings call our spirit the flesh. Hint: only choose the heavenly spirit!

Sometimes discernment is used to delay an action. Jesus revealed this in the parable of the wheat and tares or weeds. They existed together until the harvest when they were separated, a preview of the final judgment of mankind.

The examples show that discernment involves choosing one cause or belief over another or determining which spirit is involved. The word comes from the Latin *discernere* and means to separate. The usual application is to mentally "discern" good from evil. As we will see later, other than prophecies in sacred scripture, every modern prophecy should be discerned.

Among the gifts, it is easy to confuse discernment, faith, and wisdom as they seem to overlap each other. While discernment is separating good from evil, faith is not a judgmental call. It is the absolutely solemn belief that God will do a particular action. Wisdom is not a separation nor a firm belief, but rather infused knowledge that would not be known otherwise. This is different knowledge than the gift of knowledge which is frequently used in healing. Let's take a knee being healed. The knowledge could be one word, "knee" or a picture of a knee or a pain in the knee of the proclaimer.

Before we leave discernment, here's an example I know you have experienced. You walk into a church service and you feel the heaviness, or in another place, you feel uplifted. That is your spirit reacting to the ambiance.

CHAPTER 11

WISDOM

HEAVENLY-GIVEN KNOWLEDGE

We all know someone we can approach for advice. We also know well-educated people who are impractical except in their own field. I remember a fellow college student who was a genius in his field but was not conversant in anything else. However, we want to examine heavenly wisdom not worldly wisdom.

Paul comments on worldly wisdom, "For the wisdom of this world is absurdity with God" (1 Corinthians 3:19). Paul also explains that the world did not come to know God through worldly wisdom (1 Corinthians 1:21a). Here is an example: instead of looking upward and around at creation, man came up with evolution. Paul repeated something from David's work: "The Lord knows the thoughts of men and they are in vain" (Psalm 94:11).

As Christians, the knowledge we seek is the spiritual gift of wisdom. Moses, David, Solomon and Ezekiel among others were noted for their spiritual wisdom. For a further study of wisdom, the entire Book of Proverbs is about wisdom.

How do we obtain heavenly wisdom? As we have seen earlier, it is one of the gifts of the Holy Spirit. In his letter, James gives us the clue that if we lack wisdom, we should ask God for it as he gives it generously and ungrudgingly (James 1:5).

For further explanation, we return to Paul's letters. In the epistle to the Ephesians he states, "Do not continue in ignorance, but try to discern the will of the Lord" (Ephesians 5:15). Here there are two gifts involved, discernment and wisdom. Once we learn God's will, we have heavenly wisdom.

While there are many scriptural examples of this gift, there is one subtle example. Jesus was confronted by the spy zealots of his day with a quandary. But first they had to butter him up with flattery: "Teacher, we know that your words and your doctrine are completely forthright, that you are no respecter of persons but teach the way of God in truth." Then came the trap, "May we pay tax to the emperor?" If Jesus replied negatively or positively, they would be able say, "Gotcha!" But, Jesus recognized their duplicity and replied enlightened with the gift of wisdom. Since the head and face of Caesar was on the Roman coin, he should receive what is his. Likewise, God should receive what is his. This incredible wisdom floored them and they slunk away.

Another example of wisdom happened during a Sunday service. The speaker was talking about love and used John 5:19 where Jesus said, "I solemnly assure you, the Son cannot do nothing by himself. He can only do what he sees the Father doing. For whatever the Father does, the Son does likewise." As I will explain below, I learned that this was a veiled statement of the Trinity.

As I was looking at these words on the large screen, the Holy Spirit inspired me that Jesus could not see the Father with his human eyes as the Father is a Spirit. I thought that's right and couldn't wait to get home and examine the Greek word for "see".

I found a Greek/English website and with a lexicon in the public domain. Sure enough, the main meaning was to see something with the eyes or to have the power of seeing. Other meanings were, "To see with the mind's eye" and "To discover by use, to knowingly experience. These latter definitions partially answered the **how**. But, there was still a problem as Jesus took the form of a slave according to the second chapter in Philippians. Furthermore, Psalms 8:6 says, "You have made him (the Son of Man), a little less than the angels." Therefore, Jesus was fully human and could not originally perceive things in the spirit. Things changed radically in the Jordan River with the advent of the Holy Spirit on Jesus. This answers how Jesus could perceive or "see" what the Father was doing. It shows that Jesus was able to **see** the Father's actions by the power of the Holy Spirit.

CHAPTER 12

KNOWLEDGE

GOD'S ENLIGHTENMENT

The gift of knowledge is generally enlightenment about a person or situation. It can be a feeling; thought; word; vision; or any number of ways the Holy Spirit communicates his word.

My experience started in the meetings of a charismatic prayer group. The word or voice in my head for a particular healing was very loud when I was initially used for this gift. Over the years the anointing voice got softer and softer. I still plead with the Lord to talk louder. The healing was always announced to the people and sometimes multiple people were healed of the same malady. Sometimes the healing was indicated by an exact pain, for example in my knee. At other times it was an understanding, but this is hard to explain. The best example of this is a page in a book. Instead of knowing it line by line or sentence by sentence, I could understand the entire page or the vision at once.

The word I most remember was the night that I proclaimed that someone was being healed of brain cancer. Wow, what a reaction. It wasn't among the people, but among the elders. After the meeting the confrontation started as they asked me, "Didn't I know this person was in the audience?" I said, "NO." Then they asked, "Didn't I know he had brain cancer?" Once again, I said, "NO." To me it was no different than a left knee being healed; or a headache; or an arm pain. It was the anointing and the voice of the Holy Spirit speaking healing. The important thing was his same voice and the anointing, not the problem. Praise God, he **was** healed that night. It was confirmed by an MRI or an x-ray within a few days that didn't show any cancer!

I also experienced this gift in a prayer room ministry. As the person approached my prayer partner and I, many times the Holy Spirit would "clue us in" that the stated problem by the prayee was not the real problem. Often, the real problem would be indicated to us but we never mentioned it directly. You have seen it on TV programs where a person says to the doctor, "My sister has a problem I'd like to discuss." What they really mean is that they have this problem themselves, but do not want to embarrass themselves. In the prayer room ministry, we would ask general questions to try and get the person to turn to the real problem.

Sometimes it involved deliverance. Sometimes it involved a word of comfort. Sometimes the explanation was revealed in a vision. It is a beautiful experience when praying for or with someone to know the Holy Spirit is guiding you to exhibit his love. It is even more wonderful when they are slain in the Spirit or rest in the Lord, but more about that later.

We were at a charismatic conference in Phoenix and experienced this gift. In middle of his presentation, the speaker stopped and gave a word of knowledge. He proclaimed that someone's left shoulder was being healed. Just before the trip, my wife had been diagnosed with severe problems in her left shoulder. With the proclamation, she was instantly healed and was able to enjoy the rest of the conference and afterward without any pain. More importantly, she never needed nor had surgery for her arm.

In the initial prayer group, one of the ladies had a wonderful experience as she was driving. Suddenly, an inner voice said, "Pray".

She said, "Yes, Lord, I'll pray; but for who or what shall I pray?" The Lord responded, "Pray for those who are about to become involved in a certain car accident." She continued to pray and several miles later, she was hit from the right rear as she made a turn. Upon stopping to access damage, a group of unruly, screaming teenagers flew out of the second car. Among the group, the angriest was the teen age driver. The confrontation was classic. She said, "This is the seventh time I've been hit and this car is for sale. I had to show it today, and now *you* have damaged it. Admit it was your fault." The teenagers increased their anger and the group was getting out of hand.

The lady calmly retreated to her car and noted how agitated and angry they had become. She prayed, "Lord, make me calm". He did and then told the lady to get her papers and prophetically said, "You will be in command when the officer arrives." Obviously, she was proven not guilty. The example shows that God is truly in charge of every situation when we turn to him. Note that she didn't succumb to fear. Also note how many gifts were in operation starting with a word of knowledge.

At a conference, I became involved in praying for people. I was in the audience when the speaker, who I knew, said something like, "Jerry would you come and pray with people on the other side of the stage? The cause was a long line of people who wanted prayer. Fr. Bob DeGrandis later told me that he had asked me due to a word of knowledge. The Lord who gave the word also anointed both of us and the people were touched. This seems like a timely introduction to the next gift which is healing.

CHAPTER 13

HEALING

IMPROVING BODY, MIND, AND SOUL

Healing seems to be a generic word as there are so many types. Probably everyone over 25 needs some type of healing. It may be physical, emotional, mental, economic, inner, familial, or others. However, the main emphasis today seems to be physical healing and/or inner healing. The latter is really the healing of bad memories or un-forgiveness. Of course everyone wants to be well. The ultimate wellness is to be alive, active and healthy. One of my favorite comments about Jesus is that he never preached at a funeral. He just raised them from the dead.

Considering the American medical scene of rampant sicknesses like cancer, dementia, anorexia, kidney problems and others, it is amazing that the church is so quiet about the gift of healing. After all, it is really a commandment of Jesus. He not only exercised this gift thus teaching his followers, He commanded them to go forth and heal the sick. Furthermore, he said they would receive power when the Holy Spirit had come upon them. This same gift is available for all Christians. So many say that they could not heal anyone, so they don't pray for anyone. What nonsense! No one can heal anyone except Jesus, but he does want us to lay hands on people and pray that he would heal them. If they aren't healed, they at least might feel God's love.

There are so many testimonies of people being healed today primarily in Africa and South America where the people seem to be more receptive. I remember attending my local U.S. church for about 12 years and attending monthly blessings and anointing with oil. I never saw or heard of anyone being healed because they never heard about the gifts and the ministers just performed the monthly ritual. I don't think they believed in healing either. I did because I received many healings.

Some years ago I was healed of a blocked heart when people laid hands on me and prayed for me the day before the operation. Surprise; there was the original X-Ray showing the blockage and another showing that everything was normal. Praise God. I asked if I could share this wonderful news in the church monthly ritual healing service to give the folks hope and encouragement. I was refused.

I also experienced another type of healing involving smoking. While I didn't start until college, the addiction remained for many years. Of course when I started, it was cool to smoke. Later when the problems were noted, I tried to quit. I had many off and back on periods. At one time, the kids said, "Daddy, will you smoke again? You're crabby."

Unfortunately, nothing worked. One day I was sitting alone in the living room and just gave up. I said, "Lord I can't handle this and I give it to you." Immediately, there was a burning in my chest as if the Lord was burning all the tar away. I was able to take a huge breath and never smoked again, no, not even once. I had not remembered Peter's advice, "Cast your cares upon the Lord" (1 Peter 5:7).

CHAPTER 14

MIRACLES

GOD'S INTERVENTION INTO THE NATURAL WORLD

What is a miracle? I doubt that anyone needs their dictionary to realize that a miracle is beyond nature, a heavenly involvement and unexplainable. Clearly, most people are aware of the miracles worked by Jesus, but may not be as familiar as those worked by others.

One of the most notable is when Moses beheld the Egyptian army thundering through the Red Sea after his people and he complained to God to do something. God must have astounded Moses when he said something as, "You do something" (Exodus 14:16)

In the New Testament Jesus said we would work greater miracles than him.

How can this be true? During the life of Jesus, He was in a small area of what is now Israel. The preaching of Jesus was extended worldwide as his disciples traveled outward from Jerusalem. As the church grew, miracles increased in number.

How are we supposed to work miracles? Once you understand the depth of this question, you will arrive at a great love story. At first glance the answer seems to generate another question. For if Jesus was God, then for us to work greater miracles, does that mean we have to become godlike? Obviously, this cannot be true. Therefore, our task is to imitate Jesus and how he began his ministry.

The question is how did Jesus work miracles? The usual answer is, "Well, he was God wasn't He?" Surprisingly, the reply is both yes and no. Of course, he was God, but he put his divinity aside when he became man. St. Paul comes to the rescue and explains this quandary. In the letter to the Philippians, he explains how the Son of God became man just like us: "Your attitude should be the same as that of Christ Jesus who, being in the very nature of God, did not consider equality with God something to be grasped, but made himself nothing, taking the very nature of a servant, being made in human likeness. And being found in appearance as a man, he humbled himself and became obedient to death—even death on a cross" (Philippians 2:6-8 NIV).

This shows that Jesus put aside his godly self and became fully man. Note, *fully man,* for God obviously cannot be killed. Could the creator of everything be killed by an army or one of his creatures? Of course not—unless he emptied himself of his divinity which is exactly what Paul is saying in this letter.

In another letter, Paul repeats this, but in a simpler way that for a little while, Jesus was made lower than the angels (Hebrews 2:9a). However, he is now crowned with glory and honor because he suffered this death, death on a cross. Paul is repeating a praise of King David in the Psalms where he says, "What is man that you should be mindful of him, or the Son of Man (Jesus Christ) that you should care for him? You have made him little less than the angels, and crowned him with glory and honor" Psalm 8:5-6). David is prophetically saying that since Jesus accepted human stature and even death, the Father would restore his glory and honor after his death which was atonement for our sins and restoring the relationship with God lost by our forefathers in Eden.

On earth, the Son of God became the Son of Man, fully like us in every way except sin. If he hadn't put his Godly existence aside, how could he receive something he already had? He began his public ministry and worked various miracles by the power of the Holy Spirit.

As Jesus received the baptism of the Holy Spirit, this later was his gift to us. It was our personal Pentecost whereby we receive the baptism of the Holy Spirit and the resultant gifts and fruit of the Holy Spirit.

The gift of miracles is the most fascinating of the nine charisms. It is also the most well-known and coveted, as least as far as healing is concerned. The Roman Catholic Church uses the evidence of miracles in the process of determining the sainthood of a person. Looking upon miracles as only involving physical healing is too restrictive. The reason is that a miracle is a sovereign act of God and can involve anything he created. However, healing miracles are widespread throughout the world. Perhaps the most notable are the people being raised from the dead in Africa and South America. That has to be the ultimate healing. I once heard a humorous comment attributed to Lazarus as he came out of the tomb saying, "Oh no; I've got to experience death all over again."

Can you photograph a miracle? I did. I was praying on our back deck one morning before sunrise. Suddenly there was a light on the slight hill beyond our deck. I looked over the railing and there was a wreath of flowers lit in this light. They were the beautiful yellow-orange Mexican Bird of Paradise. In fact, every else was still in darkness. The flowers usually are a clump at the end of a stalk. These were a band of them brought together and arranged like a wreath or a car tire. I took it as the handiwork of God. I said, "Thank you, Father." I photographed that wonderful arrangement before the flowers returned to their natural position and have the photo on my desk as a reminder of his love.

Another miracle happened in our house. We had redone our kitchen cabinets and ACE recommended polyurethane for a finish coat. We bought a can and my wife and I applied it. We thought a second coat would be good but waited a few weeks. As we got ready, I put the paint can on the left and the brushes on the right. Opening the can, we had forgotten that we used most of it with the first coat. There was only a little bit left in the bottom of the can. Oh well, we thought we would start and at least see if we had enough for the cabinet doors. Praying in tongues all along, I turned to the right and picked up a brush. As I turned to the left to put it into the can, I noted that in those few milliseconds the Lord had given us a full can. Praise God; we had enough to finish our kitchen.

Miracles didn't stop with the early church. Many types of miracles are happening quite often in the Evangelical/Pentecostal churches and are reported on Christian television programs.

CHAPTER 15

FAITH

THE BELIEF THAT MOVES MOUNTAINS

You might ask what this gift is about, as I already have the Christian faith. Congratulations. That was faith in action, but this is a special gift of faith, a super belief in God that he will perform a particular action. It is not standing in a rigid position with fists clenched and trying to summon the courage to believe. "Faith is confident assurance concerning what we hope for, and conviction about things we do not see" (Hebrews 11:1).

Jesus outlined this gift as, "Put your trust in God. I solemnly assure you, whoever says to this mountain, 'Be lifted up and thrown into the sea, and has no inner doubts, but believes that what he says will happen, shall have it done for him.' I give you my word, if you are ready to believe that you will receive whatever you ask for in prayer, it shall be done for you" (Mark 11:23).

The immediate thought is that who could ever have this much faith? The mountain is a metaphor that Jesus used to impress upon us the necessity of belief. Elsewhere, Jesus also used the metaphor of the mustard seed, one of the smallest seeds to explain such a small faith.

One of the most striking examples of faith is the narration about Abraham having confidence when he was about to sacrifice his son. His instructions to the porters who climbed with them tell the story. He said, "Wait here until we **both** come back." He had such confidence that God would not let his son be taken regardless of what happened.

Another example involved Isaiah. There was a contest between Isaiah and 450 prophets of Baal. The two combatants prepared an animal sacrifice and called upon their god or gods to send fire. No matter how the numerous prophets of the false gods prayed or cried out, there was no fire from heaven to immolate their sacrifice. Should I add, "Advantage, Isaiah?"

To demonstrate the one, true God, Isaiah built and filled a water trench around his altar and sacrifice. God boldly answered his prayer in faith as heavenly fire consumed everything.

Another time Isaiah called for the rain to stop and later to begin. Faith is a God-given confidence that when prayed with this gift, things will happen as asked. Paul defined faith as, "Confident assurance concerning what we hope for, and conviction about things we do not see" (Hebrews 11:1). For a complete treatise of faith, read the entire 11th chapter of Hebrews.

In a humorous vein, we live about a mile from the Catalina Mountains. While Jesus talked about moving mountains, we really don't want them to move as the prevailing light and clouds present a different scene every day. God's glory is so infinite that these mountains continually reflect it in diverse colors, shadows, and shapes.

CHAPTER 16

FRUIT OF THE SPIRIT

HEAVENLY PERSONALITY HELPS

I like to sit on the back deck and soak up a few sun vitamins every now and then. One day as I was sitting there, I was thinking about the fruit of the Spirit and why are they necessary? Almost immediately, the Holy Spirit prompted me to the words of Jesus to his followers, "You are the light of the world" (Matthew 5:14). Another time I became aware that we are the temple of God (1 Cor.3:16) and that Jesus wants to present us to the Father holy, pure, and blameless (Col.1:22).

Therefore, the fruit of the Spirit is important for our continued growth in the spiritual life as they make us more Christ-like and enable us to utilize the charismatic gifts in a more loving manner. Paul lists them in Galatians 5:22 as: love, joy, peace, patient endurance, kindness, generosity, faith, mildness, and chastity.

Note, these are not the fruits (plural) of the Spirit but the fruit of the Spirit as they all work together to improve us.

Closely allied to the fruit of the Spirit are the virtues revealed throughout the scriptures. As an example, Paul states forcibly, "Instead (of false pursuits), seek after integrity, piety, faith, love, steadfastness, and a gentle spirit" (1Timothy 6:11b).

There are many other virtues of the Spirit. Here is an example of obedience. My wife and I had just walked through the Roman Forum and were sitting near the Coliseum in Rome. We were watching a man dressed as a Roman soldier of the first century. This was quite an experience sitting where we were and viewing what could have been in Paul's time.

While the man was costumed as an ancient soldier, the opportunity for tourists was to have their picture taken with him.

As we watched, a group of teenage boys had their picture taken. However, once they received the photo they ran away without paying. The soldier was quite angry and shouted to them.

As we viewed this happen, the Lord spoke to me and said, "Give him the money in your right pocket." My thought was, "Who said that?" The Lord is patient and repeated his request.

I approached the man and said that we had seen what happened. He said that he could not pursue them as the imitation Roman boots were just leather wrapped around his feet. I gave him the money and said that perhaps this would help him. He was pleased and said I could pose with him for a free photograph. I replied that was not why I gave him the money; said, "God bless you and have a nice day."

I no sooner sat down by my wife when the accuser started with his tirade that I should have given the gospel message, should have spoken of salvation and so on. My thought was that I did what I was told to do.

Peter advises us, "To undergird your virtue with faith; your discernment with virtue; and your self-control, in turn, should lead to perseverance, and perseverance to piety, and piety to care for your brother, and care for your brother, to love" (2 Peter 1:5-7).

One of the most wonderful attributes is holiness. It is also a Godly decree, "For I the Lord am your God and you shall make and keep yourselves holy because I am holy" (Leviticus 11:44-NIV). God sent his Son to re-establish this attribute. Scripture says, "But now Christ has achieved reconciliation for you in his mortal body by dying so as to present you to God holy, free of reproach and blame" (Colossians 1:22).

Jesus defined such holiness with the Beatitudes described in Matthew 5:3-12 (NIV).

- "Blessed are the poor in spirit, for theirs is the kingdom of heaven.
- "Blessed are those who morn, for they shall be comforted.
- "Blessed are the meek, for they shall inherit the earth.
- "Blessed are they who hunger and thirst for righteousness, for they will be filled, for they will be filled.
- "Blessed are the merciful, for they will be shown mercy.
- "Blessed are the pure in heart, for they will see God.
- "Blessed are the peacemakers, for they will be called sons of God.
- "Blessed are those who are persecuted because of righteousness, for theirs is the kingdom of heaven.
- "Blessed are you when people insult you, persecute you and falsely say all kinds of evil against you because of me. Rejoice and be glad, because great is your reward in heaven, for in the same way they persecuted the prophets who were before you."

The beatitudes are also mentioned in the sixth chapter of Luke:

- "Blessed are you who are poor, for yours is the kingdom of heaven.
- "Blessed are you who hunger now, for you will be satisfied.

- "Blessed are you who weep now, for you will laugh.
- "Blessed are you when men hate you, when they exclude you and insult you and reject you your name as evil, because of the Son of Man."

Jesus continued his teaching with some warnings:

- "Woe to you who are rich, for you have already received your comfort.
- "Woe to you who are well fed now, for you will go hungry.
- "Woe to you who laugh now, for you will morn and weep.
- "Woe to you when all men speak well of you, for that is how their fathers treated the false prophets."

There are also blessings listed in the Book of Revelation:

- "Blessed is the one who reads the words of this prophecy (Rev.1:3a-NIV).
- "Blessed are those who hear it and take it to heart what is written in it, because the time is near (Rev.1:3b-NIV).
- "Blessed are the dead who die in the Lord from now on (Rev.14:13-NIV).
- "Blessed is he who stays awake and keeps his clothes with him, so that he may not go naked and be shamefully exposed (Rev.16:15-NIV).
- "Blessed are those who are invited to the wedding supper of the lamb (Rev.19:9-NIV).
- "Blessed and holy are those who have part in the first resurrection. The second death has no power over them, but they will be priests of God and of Christ and will reign with him for a thousand years (Rev.20:6-NIV).

- "Blessed is he who keeps the words of the prophecy in this book (Rev.22:7-NIV).
- "Blessed are those who wash their robes, that they may have the right to the tree of life and may go through the gates into the city. Outside are the dogs, those who practice magic arts, the sexually immoral, the murderers, the idolaters, and everyone who loves and practices falsehood" (Rev.22:14-NIV).

Chapter 17

Other Gifts

The Nine Are Only a Start

As we discuss the many other gifts God provides, we are struck with the impossibility as so many are listed in scripture. For example Paul lists some of them as a prayer over the faithful. He hopes that the Father would grant a spirit of **wisdom** and **insight** to know him clearly; that he would **enlighten** our innermost vision that we would have **knowledge** of the great **hope** to which he has called us; the **wealth** of his glorious heritage; and the scope of his **power** in believers. (Ephesians 1:17-21). Other gifts are mentioned throughout Ephesians. But, let's move unto fuller discussions.

Everlasting Life

That our life is eternal is not our choice; it is how we were created. How we enjoy or suffer forever IS our choice. We have already examined various stages of life in this book. Hopefully, your choice has been to ask forgiveness and accept Jesus Christ as Lord and savior. Some folks don't want to believe in Christ, so they don't. However, that doesn't change God's revealed truth, or his eternal plans.

Scripture boldly examines our choices as, "The wages of sin is death, but the gift of God is eternal life in Christ Jesus, our Lord"

(Romans 6:23). "Offer yourselves to God as men who have come back from the dead to life" (Romans 6:12b).

FRIENDSHIP

Have you ever sung, "*What a Friend We Have in Jesus*? "If you did, what happened next? Did you move on to another verse or hymn in a service or actually start to contemplate the meaning of that line of the song? The reason this is important is that this friendship is the basis of Christianity which is not a religion but a relationship. And what a possible relationship!

Do you have any friends who would lay down their life for you? Jesus says this is the greatest love and this is the exact love that he had for us by sacrificing his life that we might have a new life through him.

Jesus and the apostles preached about the kingdom as Jesus came to restore the relationship that man once had with God. Just as he walked with Adam and Eve and was a friend to Moses, Jesus desires a close friendship with each of us. I don't mean a friendship based on attending a service every Sunday. I mean the kind of friendship that John talked about—a friendship where you talk to each other or one friend lays down his life for another (John 15:13). Earlier, the author of Proverbs said that whoever is a friend is always a friend (Proverbs 17:17).

Can you believe that Jesus wants to be your friend and you to be a friend to him? I had trouble believing this. It was years before I discovered this relationship with Jesus, but from his standpoint, it was there already. He asked me a few years ago why I couldn't accept his love? I thought I did. In fact I knew from the bible that God is Love and he loves everyone, so I assumed I was also included. Only later did I understand that he meant a personal relationship as friends where we talk to each other. We will examine such a friendship in Chapter 19.

Jesus has many names such as Lord, Savior, Messiah, Redeemer, King and many others which you see in print. But rarely is he ever called friend.

Consider that Jesus was like us in every way except as a sinner. As a young man, of course he had very close friends like Peter, James, and John whom he actually revealed his true self in the Transfiguration. Another time they were the only ones allowed to accompany him when he raised a twelve year old girl from the dead. He was also close to Lazarus, Martha, and Mary. Furthermore, he was close to all his disciples. On one occasion, he mentioned they were his friends. "I say to you who are my friends, Do not be afraid of those who kill the body and can do no more" (Luke 12:4).

The day before Passover, Mary, Martha, and Lazarus gave Jesus a banquet in Bethany where they lived (John 12:1-2). He told them he was going ahead to prepare a place for them in his Father's house. He then revealed the future Christian life by telling them he was in the Father and the Father was in him (John 14:10-11). Then he revealed he would send the Holy Spirit who would dwell within them and represent Jesus.

One more instance of friendship was the biblical phrase, "The disciple whom Jesus loved" (John 20:2) Since this referred to John and was in John's gospel, perhaps this was a little humble writing. The most positive statement about the love and closeness between Jesus and his disciples appears in John 15:15b. Jesus says, "I call you friends since I have made known to you all that I heard from my Father. It was not you who chose me; it was I who chose you" (John16:13-14).

God's love for friendship was revealed in the very first book of the bible. God created Adam in his image and was aware that

Adam needed a companion, so he created Eve. From the beginning, creation started with a friendly loving God.

THE ANOINTING

This is the physical perception of the presence of the Holy Spirit. It may happen when you are alone or praying by yourself or with someone. It is hard to describe, but is a lightness in the limbs or sudden warmth and the knowledge that God is there with you. When you are praying with someone, one or both may be zapped and then rest in the Spirit.

RESTING IN THE SPIRIT

This action of the Holy Spirit is also known as being slain in the Spirit. The best way to explain it is that you have a one on one with the Holy Spirit in a restful position, usually on the floor. With some people, it happens as folks are knocked to the floor. Clearly this is true of some charlatan preachers, but for the most part, this is wholly a gentle action of the Holy Spirit. In prayer, they faint or swoon to the floor.

My experience has usually been in a prayer room or prayer situation where the Holy Spirit wanted a deeper time with the person. After or during prayers, the person falls gently to the ground. In my experience, there were usually two prayer partners and one "catcher" to ensure a gentle transition.

As the prayer requester approached, I have experienced a loving word from the Holy Spirit many times that the person is afraid or concerned about being knocked down. Therefore, just blowing on them accomplished the same thing. One time in church, I had to pray about this for a while as I was told to blow on the folks behind me who we knew very well. I explained the word I received from the Holy Spirit and they said all right. One puff was all it took and they were thrown unto their seats and joyfully praised the Lord.

One of the fun times I had recently involved this holy puff. We were visiting friends and one of the parents said that they were never slain in the Spirit. I felt an anointing and asked if they would be open to being prayed over. I knew what was coming and said that I wouldn't touch them; only the power of the Holy Spirit would be involved. I tried one puff and they started rocking. Another puff did the job and they not only went down, but were out for a few minutes in a beautiful one on one with the Holy Spirit. God gets the glory, but it is wonderful to be used and trusted by him.

I had heard that some people have experienced this while watching a Christian TV show. This happened to me one night as I was standing in front of the TV and watching a very Spirit-filled show where the presence of the Lord was noticeable. Suddenly, the anointing hit me and I flew across the living room into the recliner chair. It was marvelous.

TRANSPORTED

This is a miraculous gift whereby the person is instantly transported or repositioned from one location to another. Ezekiel experienced this gift as he narrated, "The Spirit lifted me up and brought me to the east gate" (Ezekiel 43:5). After Jesus was baptized in the River Jordan, scripture says he was conducted by the Spirit into the desert for forty days where he was tempted by the evil one (Luke 4:1-2). Afterward, "Jesus returned in the power of the Spirit to Galilee" (Luke 4:14).

In the Book of Acts, Luke recounts the activity between Philip and the Ethiopian on the road from Jerusalem to Gaza. As Philip proclaimed the good news of Jesus, the traveler asked to be baptized. As they came out of the water, Philip was taken and immediately appeared in Azotus which is about half way between Gaza and Joppa. (Acts 8:39)

A modern example is praying for someone far away who is ill. Suddenly, you are at their bedside praying for the person. It's a good thing to check or confirm later. It could be a telephone call, something like, "I'm sorry you were ill. Did you get any visitors?" The person usually replies, "Yes, you were also here praying for me."

TRANSLATED

I've distinguished this from Transported which is an instantaneous movement of a person or people across a distance on earth. I've used Translated as referring to people instantly moved to heaven. There are two notable examples in the Old Testament involving Enoch and Elijah. "Then Enoch walked with God and he was no longer here for God took him" (Genesis 6:24). "As they walked on conversing, a flaming chariot and flaming horses came between them, and Elijah went up to heaven in a whirlwind" (2 Kings 2:11).

The New Testament expression is *lifted up* which is usually translated as raptured. The understanding is that the church will be raptured when the Lord comes down from heaven: "Then we the living, the survivors, will be caught up with them (the risen dead) in the clouds to meet the Lord in the air" (1 Thessalonians 4:13-18).

There is also the happening whereby a person visits heaven in the spirit temporarily and walks, seeing heavenly things, or talking with the Lord.

ANOTHER DWELLING

John tells us that Jesus dwells in us. Most Christians are aware that this is by the power of the Holy Spirit, but surprisingly, he also says we dwell in him! This passage in scripture is like a thunderclap: "When anyone acknowledges that Jesus is the Son of God, God dwells in him and him in God" (1 John 4:15). To make sure we understand this, John rephrases this in the second part of the next verse: "God is love and he who abides in love, abides in God and God in him" (1 John 16b).

THE GIFT OF DANCE

Most people are familiar with the fact that David danced before the Lord (2 Sam. 6:14). There was also an earlier reference in Exodus. After their deliverance from their enemies through the Red Sea, Moses led the Israelites in a song of praise. Mirian and the women took their tambourines and danced and sang to the Lord. (Exodus 15:20-21).

There are numerous references to dance particularly in the Old Testament. When Saul and David returned after slaying the Philistine, women came out from all the cities of Israel singing and dancing as they greeted them (1 Sam. 18:6). "Let them praise him in the festive dance" (Psalm 149:3) and "Praise him with timbrel and dance" (Psalm 150:4). "You changed my mourning into dancing" (Psalm 30:12a). Another joyous example happened when they were transporting the Ark of the Covenant: "While David and all Israel danced before God with great enthusiasm, amid songs and music on lyres, harps, tambourines, cymbals, and trumpets" (1 Chronicles 13:7-8).

There have been times in church when I could sense the choreography of the Holy Spirit as the dance was so anointed. I remember the look on one dancer's face. It showed that she was dancing before the throne of our Lord and not just in the front of the church.

PRIESTLY KINGDOM

When Moses and God spoke on Mount Sinai, this was clearly a prophetic acclamation as well a gift: "You shall be to me a kingdom of priests, a holy nation. That is what you must tell the Israelites" (Exodus 19:6). To make sure the early Christians understood this, Peter expanded the earlier proclamation in Exodus, "You, however, are a chosen race, a royal priesthood, a holy nation, a people he claims for his own to proclaim the glorious works of the one who called you from darkness into his marvelous light" (1 Peter 2:9). Peter reiterates this as applying to the Christian peoples as a holy priesthood offering spiritual sacrifices to God through Jesus Christ (1 Peter 2:5b).

ETERNAL LIFE

"I have written this to you to make you realize that you possess eternal life—you who believe in the name of the Son of God" (1 John 5:13). This certainly is tied to the gift of salvation: "For God so loved the world that He gave his only begotten Son so that whoever believes in him has everlasting life" (John 3:16). Note the verb tense. As a person becomes saved or born again, choosing Jesus Christ as Lord and Savior, they begin eternal life while still on earth. Do you understand this? Most people don't when they say, "I hope I'll go to heaven".

SURPRISES

Our heavenly Father likes to surprise his children just as we do something for our children. Sometimes his surprise gift is some gold fleck or a gemstone. People also report a marvelous fragrance. We have experienced this sweet smell in our living room on occasion and usually blurt out, "Oh, the angels are here. Welcome. Praise God." We've also seen angels in churches and my wife has experienced one as a travel companion for a few miles. They always seem to be tall, wearing a white robe with a golden sash or belt. The one surprise we have heard about but never experienced is the sudden, instantaneous loss of 20 or more pounds. We need this gift!

These examples aren't something to focus upon but events to strengthen our faith in our God who loves us. You've heard the phrase, "Seek the giver, not the gift."

INFUSED SKILLS

In the book of Exodus, The Lord told Moses that he had gifted Bezalel with a divine spirit of skill and understanding and knowledge in every craft. These included the production of embroidery; fabricating gold, silver and bronze items; in cutting and mounting precious stones; carving wood and every other craft. Furthermore, the Lord endowed all the experts with the necessary skills to make the items used in worship. (Exodus 31: 1-11).

HOLY SPIRIT NUDGES

I've known for a long time that the Holy Spirit has a sense of humor. In some conversations, I've made a comment that sometimes makes people laugh, but I've never figured out why. The answer is that the Holy Spirit knows just the appropriate injection.

Just recently, we had a forecast for strong cold weather and a rain storm on the local TV stations. Therefore, when my wife returned from work, I felt led to rush outside with an umbrella. We both laughed as it was 75 degrees and a beautiful sunny day. Where did the idea come from? It wasn't from me!

Recently in the dentist's chair I had him and his nurse assistant laughing all the time, but it wasn't from things I had ever said before; they just came. Perhaps they were having a bad day and needed a lift.

Since the Holy Spirit is so loving, I've experienced nudges to do loving things for my wife that I wouldn't have thought about by myself.

EXAMPLES OF GOD'S LOVE

We were on the ocean shoreline with another couple in a two bedroom rental condo for a long weekend. We had enjoyed the view, the beach and especially the fresh fish and shrimp. Our last night there, we going to cook in the condo and eat on the balcony. That afternoon we walked along the beach and stopped at the beach vendors by the condo and bought some nice jewelry. Just before supper, I sensed the Holy Spirit saying, "I want you to go downstairs and pray for the two ladies at the beach vendors". I then thought how am I going to explain this to avoid a laugh or comment from the other couple? Sometimes God operates behind the scenes and is subtle but is always in charge. Other times, he is absolutely apparent in what he does. As I was thinking of what to say, the other husband suddenly asked if I had any music CD's in our car downstairs? He could have asked this any time before, any day or night. I almost laughed out loud for our Lord not only tells us what he wants; he arranges it. I didn't need to mention a reason to go downstairs. I went for the music disks we had in the car, but first went to the vendors and asked if they were open for prayer. They were and everything worked out including the sweet guitar music we played during dinner which made the fresh fish taste even better.

YOU THE READER

In 1986, the Lord spoke to me and said that he had shared many gifts with me and still had many more to give, but did I realize the greatest gift was myself? Wait! This doesn't have anything to do with me nor is it an ego trip, but is the revelation that we are created in his image and **each** one of us is to reflect his glory in a special way. It also shows his generosity. Here are some verses to magnify this teaching and from a derived meaning to show why abortion is abhorrent:

- "I have written your name on the palms of my hand (Isaiah 49:16).
- "Your names are inscribed in heaven (Luke 10:20).
- "You created my innermost being; you knit me in my mother's womb (Psalm 139:13).
- "Your eyes have seen my actions; in your book they are all written; my days were limited before one of them existed (Psalm 139:16).
- "You have been my guide since I was formed, my security at my mother's breast. To you I was committed at birth; from my mother's womb you are my God (Psalm 22:10-11).
- "I give you thanks that I am fearfully, wonderfully made (Psalm 139:14).

- "Before I formed you in the womb, I knew you (Jeremiah 1:5).
- "As for you, every hair of your head has been counted (Matthew 10:30).
- "We are his offspring (Acts 17:28).
- "Before all ages, in the beginning, he created me, and through all ages I shall not cease to be" (Sirach 24:9).

1 John 3:1b states, "The reason the world does not recognize us is that it never recognized the Son." I added a note in my bible asking, "Do we recognize ourselves?" Now do you realize the impact of God saying, "The greatest gift is yourself?" Remember, you have God's DNA and he lives in you. Each of us has been gifted in different ways to reflect his glory. "Whatever you do—you should do all for the glory of God." (1 Cor.10:31b).

VISITATIONS PART 1

A visitation is one of the most wonderful gifts. Imagine the creator visiting his creature. Imagine an angelic visit. Now imagine Jesus himself visiting you. The first book of the Bible, The Book of Genesis, established God's wishes for a relationship with man. This was later confirmed with others, but especially with Moses at numerous times.

After the resurrection, Jesus returned to friendship with his disciples even eating with them. Throughout history, there have been instances where Jesus appeared to people. Today there are many stories of this happening in the Mideast.

I experienced a life changing event. Jesus suddenly appeared before me one day and introduced himself by saying, "Hello". I was stunned. This wasn't a vision, a dream, or an apparition. He literally stood before me and talked with me and showed me heavenly things.

I wondered afterward why I didn't kneel before him. The reason I didn't was that I couldn't move as I was so struck by the love just pouring from his eyes. Any words I use to describe our Lord are meaningless compared to his physical presence.

There have been many modern prophecies that in these last days, angels will come forth and there will be many heavenly visitations.

I understand we are to consider the things of heaven more than worldly things according to scripture, but sometimes we can get too serious about our religion. My wife and I were at a very Spirit-filled conference in Tucson when we smelled coconuts which were an impossible scent in a conference hall. We wondered if there were angels around as in our living room. We recognized our pastor's daughter sitting near us. At a break, my wife asked her what she was doing. She replied, "Oh, I just rubbed my hands with coconut oil!" My wife told her the story and laughingly exclaimed, "You are my coconut angel."

VISITATIONS PART 2

In Part One, we discussed heavenly visitors. In this Part, we'll talk about something not many of us have considered. Perhaps, some folks have thought, "Oh, I can't wait until I get to heaven." Well, you are partly there already. When you became born again, eternity began for you; it's just that you are temporarily earthbound. However, we will examine how it may be possible to visit heaven in the spirit now. Stay with me and I'll show you some of the scriptures that show this. In the meantime, consider that Paul and John described their heavenly visitations.

1). God dwells in believers who acknowledge that Jesus is the Son of God and we dwell in God (1 John 4:15).

2). Since we are risen with Christ, we are to seek heavenly things where Christ sits at the right hand of God (Colossians 3:1).

3). We are to be intent on heavenly things rather than earthly things. (Colossians 3:2).

4). We are fellow citizens of the saints and members of the household of God (Ephesians 2:19).

5). We should approach the heavenly throne with confidence (Hebrews 4:16).

6). Jesus has bestowed on us every spiritual blessing in the heavens (Ephesians 1:3).

7). Jesus stated that no one can enter God's kingdom without being begotten of water and the Spirit (John 3:5).

Doesn't it follow that if you are born again and Spirit-filled, you can enter God's kingdom following the words of Jesus? Praying these scriptures, at times I have asked the Holy Spirit to take me to heaven. In the spirit, I have prayed and adored him and spoke in tongues. Sometimes he said, "Let's walk" and showed me aspects of heaven.

It is hard to describe the colors of heaven. Saying they are more vivid doesn't convey the reality. In addition there are colors I've never seen before. One time I saw a fusion of maroons, blues, reds, and others come together in a new color for my eyes. I felt the awesome power of God and blurted out, that color is ramoon. Regardless of heavenly scenes, nothing compares to seeing our Lord as King magnificently sitting upon his throne.

DIVERS TONGUES

This is another form of praying in tongues. The best example is Pentecost (Acts 2:1-12) where the apostles and disciples spoke in tongues and the people heard them in their own language.

I've had this experience. Once, I felt the anointing as I was directed to an Asian lady. I asked her and she was agreeable for prayer. As I started to pray vocally, there was a sudden shift into an oriental language. The Holy Spirit gave the inflections and vocal rhythms. When I finished, she said that it was a beautiful prayer and she felt peaceful and joyous.

She said "You were speaking in Chinese. Do you think you have a mission to the Chinese people?" I replied that I didn't even know how to say hello in Chinese. She said, "Well you just prayed in Chinese so you must speak it." Once again, I repeated that it was the Lord blessing her in her language and I was speaking with the gift of tongues; it was not my language. She countered with, "But you just spoke it!"

INTERCESSORY PRAYER

This is a beautiful gift which comes from the Latin, meaning to go between. What do we intercede about? We could pray for a sick friend or family member, a situation, for peace, or our government leaders. Here in the Southwest, we frequently pray for rain to minimize our usual drought. We truly need God to help us so there are a myriad of things to ask. In fact, Timothy states, "First of all, I urge that petitions, prayers, intercessions, and thanksgiving be offered for all men, especially for kings and those in authority, that we may lead undisturbed and tranquil lives in perfect piety and dignity" (1 Timothy 2:1-2).

There are numerous examples of such encouragement for intercessory prayer in scripture. Luke reminded us to always pray without losing heart (Luke 18:1). James advised us to pray for one another (James 5:16). Paul is somewhat stronger in his advice as he states, "Never cease praying" (1 Thessalonians 5:17). Paul also reminds us that when we don't know how to pray, the Holy Spirit intercedes for us as God himself wills (Romans 8:26-27).

As we showed, it is God's will that we all pray and pray often. There are some folks whom the Lord has blessed with the gift of intercessory prayer. Many times, I said, "Wow, I wish I could pray like that." My prayers are usually short or in tongues. The gifted can pray in many ways. Here are some examples (name edited) of intercessory prayers from friends who have this gift.

"Lord, I ask right now that XXX be found and that he's okay. Let him get in touch with his mother, letting her know that he is well. I ask for your angels assigned to him to get him to a place where he can be taken care of and for his whereabouts to be known. In the meantime, Lord, I ask that XXX allow you to turn his life around. May he be given strength to say no to the lifestyle he is living. Lord, this is going to take your deliverance power to touch him even now and to set him free. I speak freedom to XXX!

XXX, I call you forth. I take authority over the spirits that have you bound. I command *them* bound and broken off your life and I say, 'Be free!' And now, Lord, grant your power to come on him. Raise him up whole, healed, and delivered by the power of Jesus Christ. Protect him and get him to a place where he can get help. Let a police officer or someone who sees him recognize that he needs medical assistance, (if that be the case), so he can receive it. Thank you, Lord. Comfort his mother's heart; Holy Spirit; let her know that you were there and you heard her prayers concerning her son. Bless her and bless her son. I ask this in the name of Jesus. Amen."

Another friend learned about a need and lifted the burden to the Lord who gave her the words and method to pray for the situation. Recently she was praying for a friend's son who has been tormented in his mind. She said, "The Holy Spirit gave me a vision of our Lord and Savior, Jesus Christ, with a crown of thorns piercing his head with the blood spilling down his face and neck. Then I heard that this was the healing for all mental sickness. I immediately started to intercede for XXXX with the blood of Jesus coming from the crown of thorns on Jesus' head which is healing for the mind of XXXX. I also reminded the enemy that when two or three are united in one accord, that which is asked for, comes to pass. So I bound the spirit of mental illness, the spirit of imbalance, the spirit of depression, the spirit of discouragement, and the spirit of eastern religions to break its power off him and for a sound mind, power and love to be revealed to him in Jesus' name. I prayed to break off the orphan spirit and that the power of God's Sonship would come into his mind and heart in Jesus' name. Amen

Another friend prayed for a couple who needed physical healing. "Father God, you are so worthy and I praise you and thank you for all that you are doing. Lord, I ask that you would place your hands on XX and make his wrist whole again. I ask that all pain and inflammation go now in the mighty name of Jesus."

Another example: "Lord, I lift up XXX and ask you to touch her and that all pain in her back and legs will be gone now in Jesus' name. Lord, pour out your oil from heaven and oh, Holy Spirit, come now and touch the both of them; fill them right now and send your ministering angels to both of them. Comfort them; fill them with your joy, Lord, in the mighty, powerful and glorious name of Jesus. Amen."

These examples are from experienced intercessors. For most of us, "Jesus, help" works just as well since we don't always know the details.

One of our human frailties is to wonder if God hears our prayers. Of course he does, but maybe the answer or healing doesn't happen in our time zone. Other than prayers for an arm or leg adjustment which usually happens during prayer, I have this problem. I belong to the vending machine generation. You put a coin in the machine and a can or candy drops out. With me, the Lord's timing is much longer. I think this is a learning exercise for me to trust him.

Sometimes God knows the timing while we do not. An example I've experienced happens at stoplights. Maybe five people cross in front of me. I get the anointing to pray for a particular one or two of them and zip off a short prayer. I have to use tongues as I don't know them and age, race, gender, or size is incidental. The anointing is very specific. Another example happens more often. This is the traffic situation where someone almost causes an accident or cuts me off. At one time in my life, something inappropriate would come forth. Now, I ask the Lord to give them the wisdom to know him and the wisdom to become a good driver. Consider that God is always in charge. He is both the inspiration and the culmination of our prayers.

While we can be intercessors, there is only one mediator. "And the truth is this: God is one. One also is the mediator between God and men, the man Christ Jesus who gave himself as a ransom for all" (1 Timothy 2:5-6).

Rather than lone rangers or lone prayers, prayer intercessors are usually united with others in a church or prayer group. The initial prayer from one of the group typically goes to all of them via e-mail so an individual prayer for the person or situation is multiplied.

NUGGETS

These aren't golden nuggets, but those found in the bible. I define these as nuggets when a passage in the bible that you've read numerous times suddenly comes to life. Here are some examples:

1). Jesus said pick up your cross **daily**. I've always assumed this meant something personal or family related like a sickness. Reading that passage one day, I suddenly realized that our crosses aren't something we pick up each day; they are with us 24/7. Furthermore, we don't have just one cross; we have many that we are carrying. The cross Jesus mentions is to trust Him.

2). Matthew (1:22-25) repeats a passage from Isaiah 7:14 which says "The virgin shall be with child and give birth to a son and they shall call Him Emmanuel, a name which means 'God is with us.'" The child's name was Jesus; Emmanuel was a title or proclamation.

3). God is with us and aware of us. "For I know well the plans I have in mind for you says the Lord, plans for your welfare, not for woe! Plans to give you a future full of hope. When you call me; when you pray to me; I will listen to you" (Jeremiah 29:11-13).

THE ARMOR OF GOD

In Ephesians 6:10-17, Paul uses the clothes of a Roman soldier as a defensive mode to thwart the evil one and his minions. Truth is the belt around your waist as justice is your breastplate. Your footgear is the zeal to propagate the gospel. You can hold up your faith before you as your shield from the fiery darts of the evil one. Your salvation is your helmet and the sword of the Spirit is the word of God. Remember, Jesus used scripture as his sword in defeating Satan when he tempted Jesus after the baptism in the Jordan. An interesting but not obvious fact is what Jesus quoted. It was from the Torah or Old Testament as the New Testament hadn't been written yet.

TEARS

The gift of tears needs an explanation. At first glance, it would seem that they are somehow related to an enlightened spiritual experience at a time of sorrow. My experience is just the opposite. The gift of tears is a time of extreme euphoria with tears gushing forth. My experience has always been related to good times, for example, a perception of God's creations in nature or beautiful scenery or sunsets, or listening to beautiful music and seeing God's hand in giving talent. One that never fails is Pavarotti's rendition of Puccini's Nessum Dorma. Other experiences were a little dachshund puppy licking my face or watching kittens in their crazy play antics. My reaction has always been a sudden but continuous flow of tears. The accompanying feeling is one of overwhelming joy. The event is so powerful, I usually cry out to my heavenly Father. It seems I cannot take such joy all at once.

Surprisingly, some happy story or movie endings have produced the same reaction. Evidently, the Holy Spirit is the author and the reaction is one of perceived goodness of God's greatness. I believe it is seeing God's glory in his creation or goodness personified. Technically speaking, my wife calls me a mush.

LIGHT

This gift is really amazing in the life of a Christian. And it probably dumbfounded the apostles when Jesus told them, "You are the light of the world" (Matthew 5:14a). When we realize this also pertains to us, it is quite astounding.

So they would get a clue, Jesus said that you don't put a lamp under a bushel basket so it is hidden. He then explained, "In the same way, your light must shine before men so that they may see goodness in your acts and give praise to your heavenly Father" (Matthew 5: 16). "I have come into the world as its light to keep anyone who believes in me from remaining in the dark" (John 9:46). He also warned his followers that to become sons of light, they must keep faith in the light (John 12:36).

Later, Jesus alarmed them as they waited for a conquering king by saying "The light is among you only a little longer" (John 12:35). Like each of us, they probably remembered him saying, "I am the light of the world." That is the second part of the verse. All of us have probably glossed over the first part. The entire verse is absolutely necessary for our understanding. Jesus said, "**While I am in the world**, I am the light of the world" (John 9:5). The question now becomes where is Jesus today? Is he sitting under an olive tree in Jerusalem? Obviously not; he is risen and ascended to heaven and sits at the right hand of the Heavenly Father. Jesus further stated, "No more than a branch can bear fruit of itself apart from the vine, can you bear fruit apart from me. I am the vine; you are the branches. He who lives in me and I in him will produce abundantly, for apart from Me you can do nothing" (John 15:4-5). Jesus also strongly emphasized that by not living in him, a person is like dead wood and is only good for kindling. All this rhetoric is clearly laying the groundwork for the Pentecost experience, the Baptism of the Holy Spirit. Jesus said, "You will receive power when the Holy Spirit comes down on you; then you are to be my witnesses in Jerusalem, throughout Judea and Samaria, yes even to the ends of the earth" (Acts 1:8).

How are we to be his light to the world? By the same Baptism of the Holy Spirit where Jesus lives in us. We are the descendants of the apostles and disciples and are to carry on the work of Jesus.

Someday, while looking in the mirror, you may hear, "Well, you certainly don't look like the light of the world." Reject that negative spirit immediately, for Jesus himself gave you that approbation. Believe him.

Arm & Leg Adjustments

I imagine that your first thought is some type of push/pull technique. Rest easily; this is spiritual chiropractory.

I learned of this at a healing conference by Fr. Robert DeGrandis. Many people have a kink in their back or elsewhere from simple things like getting out of bed. This prayer usually relieves the pressure or pain.

The first step is, get the person to sit upright in a straight chair. Next, you ask them to extend their arms and bring their hands together. You are looking to see if one arm is longer than the other. However, most people will bend their arm so the finger ends are even. You have to tell them to just bring the hands together. Invariably one arm is longer than the other.

The next step is to pray in tongues or English. The short arm will either creep steadily out or will snap out. I've never experienced this movement without praying in tongues. The reason is simple as we don't know what caused the soreness, but the Holy Spirit does. Therefore, the prayer language is typically different for each person. To facilitate the prayer language, it's easiest to start in your own language. The Spirit will shift to another prayer language especially for the person. I haven't seen any success by just praying in English, but others have.

Should this procedure fail, perhaps the bad back is caused by something lower. In that case, ask them to extend their feet and note if one is longer. Hold their legs up as it is difficult for them other than just momentarily. Start praying again. Many times the legs will achieve equality or near to it. Then try the arms again. Should both methods be unfruitful, the reason may be the need for deliverance. Therefore, silently pray and bind any negative spirits.

This prayer technique is not something where you have to find someone to pray with you. If you have a bad back, find a straight chair in your home and start praying. You don't have to close your eyes as many do. I tell people, "Please keep your eyes open and watch what Jesus is going to do for you".

GOD WITHIN

Have you noticed that I haven't mentioned love as a gift? Then where did it originate? Surprisingly, love always existed. Since the Holy Trinity did not have a beginning, that is why we can say that God is love. Unlike us, God does not have a vague or fleeting love. God is love eternal.

Love comes from God. The apostle, John explains that "If anyone loves the world, the Father's love has no place in him" (1 John 2:15b). Earlier, we talked about the secular world and the spiritual world. This is the same as the teaching of Jesus that we cannot serve two masters (Matthew 6:24) If we love the worldly goods and worldly allure, we do not have our mind on God, our creator.

To love is really a commandment, first revealed by Moses in Deuteronomy 6:4-6. Jesus explained that the first commandment is to love God and the second is to love our neighbor.

Paul stressed the position of love in the Christian life. He said that if we have all the gifts except love, we have nothing. John summarizes the two great commandments strongly as, "I ask you, how can God's love survive in a man who has enough of this world's goods yet closes his heart to his brother when he sees him in need" (John 3:17)!

CHAPTER 18

DREAMS, VISIONS, AND MORE

ANOTHER WAY GOD COMMUNICATES

God has used numerous methods to communicate to all peoples, and not just his chosen people or his kingdom people. The dreams of Pharaoh and Nebuchadnezzar show this. In both cases, God's people analyzed the dreams which were warnings for the pagan monarchs. The warnings in their dreams were consistent with Job's writings. (Job 33:14-18).

One of my favorite scriptural dream references is the time God appeared and spoke to Solomon in a dream. God said, "Ask something of me and I will give it to you" (1 Kings 3:5). Wow! This was a forerunner to the statement of Jesus, "Ask and you shall receive; seek and you shall find; knock and it shall opened to you" (Luke 11:9).

Both Josephs of the Old and New Testament were involved with heavenly dreams. In the OT, Joseph was shown his future (Genesis 37:5). In the NT, it was a dream that relieved Joseph's fear about marriage to Mary, a pregnant girl. Later after the couple fled to Egypt, it was a dream that sent them back to Israel in peace. A popular verse today is Joel's prophecy that old men shall dream dreams and young men shall see visions (Joel 3:1).

I have heard that you can invite the Lord to provide dreams. The method doesn't work for me. One of the requirements is to leave pencil and paper on the night table so you can write the dream. For most people, the first priority upon waking is a visit to the bathroom.

Surely, these recommendations are meant for single people. Can you imagine turning on the light and waking your spouse? "Oh, honey you're awake; I'm just writing down the great dream I had."

Should I leave the pen and paper on the dining room table? That doesn't work for me either as I do need the bathroom sojourn. In addition, years ago, my brother made the morning comment that I had the breath of a cougar. So that needs attention when I get up. So that's two things that need to be accomplished before I become a dream scribe. Ah, there are more problems.

Since Air Force basic training, I have abandoned pajamas and sleep in my shorts. If I neglected the bathroom stop, I could head for the dining room half asleep and the writing material. Unfortunately, when I arrived I would be awake, but half frozen. In summer we leave the air conditioning on and in winter we turn the thermostat down.

Yet another problem is that I'm not cognizant until I have two cups of black coffee. In addition, this is my job every morning as I choose the different beans to combine and start the grinder and the "make the coffee" process. When my wife awakes, she always has freshly brewed coffee for her morning ritual.

Yes, these are excuses. I am aware that Job said that God speaks once or twice in a dream. David told us, "I will praise the Lord who counsels me; even at night my heart counsels me" (Psalm 16:7). The Lord has free reign to say anything, anytime he wants. If he desires to change my dream mode, that is fine. In the meantime, we are communicating as you'll see in the next chapter.

Since I haven't had any major dream experiences, I can't relate examples. I've talked to experts in the field of dreams who commented on the symbols God uses. These are usually from our experiences. For instance, a door may be open or closed. The door isn't the important part as it may suggest something happens soon or we are blocking God in a particular action.

APPARITIONS

These appearances by heavenly saintly people are well respected in the Roman Catholic Church. The popular church approved locations are well known such as Fatima, Guadalupe, and Lourdes. The recent phenomenon at Medjugorje has not been approved yet. The Virgin Mary is most popular recurrence in these apparitions.

VISIONS

Visions are described as "an experience, generally regarded as beneficent or meaningful, in which a personage, thing, or event appears vividly or credibly to the mind, although not actually present, under the influence of a divine or otherwise spiritual agency, etc." (Vision 3—Webster's Encyclopedic Unabridged Dictionary).

This confirms my experience with visions. The danger is that a picture can be self-induced from the imagination. An example of this is imagining the glory of Jesus and a picture comes to mind, perhaps of some painting depicting this. However, this is not from a heavenly gift, but from our memory. I have experienced several glory visions of Jesus and each one was different with one so incredible and vast it is difficult to describe. I've also seen visions during spirit-filled services such as seeing angels. Likewise, I have seen visions while walking in heaven. My most memorable one was confirmed two years later in scripture. I was walking on the golden road once when I noticed areas of the road turned green. Since gold doesn't corrode, I was mystified. I looked up and saw a rainbow with shades of green. The road reflected the greens. While I had read and reread the Book of Revelation, a particular verse never hit me until one day I realized that it confirmed what I had seen. The verse is Rev. 4:3b which reads, "Around the throne was a rainbow as brilliant as emerald" (i.e. green).

During Sleep

One morning I mentioned to my wife that while I went to bed after her, she was talking in her sleep. I said, "You weren't talking English and it didn't seem to be in tongues. Maybe it was Klingon." She said, "You do the same thing." Well, I haven't read anything about talking in our sleep, so I won't comment.

CHAPTER 19

COFFEE TIME

TALKING & LISTENING WITH JESUS

I met my future wife at a small church discussion group. As she came in the door, I thought that she was the most beautiful woman my age that I had seen since moving out West. Since I was near the entrance, I asked her if she would like a cup of coffee. Many years later, I still make coffee for us every morning. Since I am an early riser, I'm the coffee guy.

I get a cup before she rises and use this period as prayer time. I start with various prayers including intercessory prayers as well as praise and worship. After using my prayer language, I pray in English. One day our Lord responded and we started to talk and he said, "Let's do this again". The format is talk about the day before and the present day and then I start to ask questions. I journal my talk and his response. We talk as friends, back and forth. I'd like to share some of these conversations that I call coffee time which is coffee with Jesus. I encourage you to spend prayer time to develop a conversational relationship with our Lord with or without coffee.

We know Christianity is based on a relationship with God rather than adherence to rules and rituals. You don't have coffee each day with a stranger. Jesus Christ is not only our Lord, Savior Messiah, Redeemer, and King, but also our friend. We are the ones who haven't considered him as a friend, but a distant being. I started to know Jesus more as a friend one day when journaling his thoughts with me. He stopped talking so I stopped writing. My thought was, "How can the creator of the universe be out of breath?" Suddenly, he said, "Are you through writing already because I'm not through!" Rather than be hurt, it was like a friend elbowing me in the ribs and smiling while he kidded me. Only friends do that to each other.

Another time we were walking together in heaven and came to a waterfall. I looked at him and he had a smile on his face. He said, "Let's walk through it". Well, we did and exiting the other side both of us were perfectly dry. I looked at him and he had an expression on his face as much to say, "Hey, look what I just did". Then, he became my Lord again and said, "I want you to go back through the waterfall, turn around and come back; I will wait here for you". I did as my Lord and friend commanded. He said, "I had you do that to teach you something" and then he told me something so loving that it has affected the rest of my life. When reviewing *Gifted,* someone said, "But you never mentioned what he said". I replied, "That's right."

I looked through about eight recent months in my journal and noted that Jesus used certain words repeatedly. I also noted three themes. One was giving direction to my wife and I. Another was his quest to get folks saved and into the kingdom. The last was the pain for a world currently gone wild with sin and the forthcoming re-establishment of his glory for all to see. Time is short was another major theme.

Here are the most popular phrases from our conversations and their frequency: Fear not (42); Love (32); the kingdom (22); his glory (17); and time is short (13). My background as an engineer shows in this cryptic analysis, but is my way to show what our Lord talked about. The summary is that no matter what happens in these end times, do not be fearful for he is in charge and loves us. The Lord first said "Fear not" to Abraham and continues to say it. Perhaps fear and worry are the evil ones major weapons to take our mind off God. That's why our Lord wants us to trust him in all situations. The first two phrases used the most showed that his love conquers any fear we might have. Below, I've chosen some of his responses to me. To differentiate, I've used "**Lord**" in asking Jesus and "Son" as he replies.

"Lord, how do you see the world today?"

"Son, my people perish for lack of knowledge. The lure of the world is strong. It is so strong that people have no time for me and so many ministries have abandoned my word. I am truth, yet they seek anything but truth. For some it is a good time without any thought of the implications; their God is something physical. Foolish man; they will stand empty before me. For some it is the idol of a star to copy and imitate. How long lasting is that? Others use their mouth as a buzz saw to chop down everyone but themselves whom they see as the ideal.

"Richness covets richness; politicians covet power and endurance. Indeed they are not of this world for they have created a world all for themselves. I cannot even talk about sexuality and drugs as these are also false gods, idols, to be pursued to their demise.

"I have so much love, but who wants it when the electronic things call them? I cry for my people for they are lost and there aren't enough of my people to find them. Time is short. Do not let this be your ending as well. Seek me even closer, even deeper, and we will find each other" (11/12/10).

"Son, yes, we are friends and I pour out my heart to you. I want you both to come closer to me for I have plans for you both. Continue to listen to what I place before you. But most of all, be absolutely aware that I am with you, in you, for you, and by you. No, you are never alone: the three of us are with you and the two of you with me also makes three.

"Just think; is there anything we can't accomplish? Let no little thing or things bother you. Soon people will come to you and ask how? Be ready to tell them it is I who guide you from eternity and I can guide them also" (11/14/10).

"Son, what I have said will happen soon. I say, 'Fear not for fear will be everywhere and my people must be guiding lights. Lo, I cannot save a world turned against me and my commands. Even if you look upon them as my wishes, they are divine wishes from your God. What have they meant? Nothing! Sin is everywhere. However, I do equip my saints for my glory, for my power and salvation. Help the people who come to you and bring them into my kingdom'" (11/17/10).

"Son, for now, enjoy me and let us enjoy each other for you have still not realized my love for you. Just think of all you have received; that is from me.

"Tonight I want you to say, 'Time is short.' The kingdom cries out for new members and only my people can step forth and enlighten the darkness that is everywhere. Do not be afraid of the dark in any manner for I am the light. I have conquered darkness and will light your way by my Holy Spirit" (11/17/10).

"Son, peace is my gift to you, but look about you. Peace is a forgotten word yet everyone talks and strives for peace. The quest is among nations as well as within people, yet only I can provide the peace they seek. Will there be a change before I come? I am the Prince of Peace, but I am never sought on the global plane. How many times have I said that time is short, yet no one believes? I've said this many times in scripture. For each person, time IS short for them as no one knows their demise time.

"What is time for my people? They aren't living in time for they are already living eternally with me where there is no time" (11/19/10).

"Son, I can do all these things you ask. For now, you need patience and growth. Let me purify you while I gift you. I want you to represent me. Stretch out your arm; it is me. Remember that. It is always me who does things. Loosen up and do a little each day and you will see results. I am with you" (11/23/10).

"Lord, yesterday was wonderful. It's fun to be used by your Holy Spirit. Yesterday there was happiness in spite of strange occurrences. Today I took authority in your name."

"Son, yesterday, you glimpsed me in a new way as a playful Jesus. Remember me as a friend to all" (11/30/10).

"Lord, I have so many questions today."
"Son, you ask so many questions, but one overall thought dominates all and this is my love for you. You may not realize it, but you are constantly being trained. I see your faults and will help you. Come to me more often and rejoice that we are one. The rapture is only your physical removal, but you are already with me. You must believe that. You and I are one now, not some time in the future.

"Expect a war soon; expect more wars soon. You will see my revelation coming together as all is ready. I want you to be ready so you can explain it. It is the secular world of unbelief versus my word that has always been there for study. They didn't want to believe, so they didn't. That doesn't change my revealed truth nor my eternal plans. There will be a great awakening soon. Be strong with belief in me" (12/5/10).

"Son, don't fear; change is coming, a very big change that will affect everyone. Finally, my glory will be there for all to see" (12/9/10).

"Son, take and write 'I love you,' especially when you pray or minister together. I have called you to this yet you restrain; you hold back. Are you afraid of releasing or revealing my power? Fear not, I am with you, for you, and in you both. I want people to sense my love through you as a couple. Put aside all the claptrap you carry and get with it. Watch what happens and let your faith in me grow so you can minister to my people" (12/19/10).

"Son, why do you stay away from me? Why do you keep your distance? I live in you and you live in me. Can we be any closer? You ask for my presence. I say you already have it. Act like it. I can always be present with you and share my presence with all you meet. I won't disappoint you. Your failure is false humility. Let me be proclaimed and understood through you. I have chosen you, therefore, do my bidding. I want you to be strong with my power. You have nothing except what I gave you, but I have given you everything. Now act" (12/22/10).

"Son, I mean to help you understand and then help others. Time quickens and things will happen suddenly. Soon something momentous will happen, but no one is prepared except my people. Then you must reflect my glory and my kingdom to all. Remember, this word of mine is soon" (1/5/2011).

"Lord, I messed up; help me."
"Son, you were foolish to depart from me like a little child. Am I not creator of the universe? Now I welcome you back and forgive you. Go in peace and stay in peace, my peace" *(3/1/2011).*

"Son, you worry too much and your trust is so low. I am not always a God of immediacy but slow in order to bring trust. I give you both hope that all will be well. Your times are not yet done, far from it; you haven't begun" (3/7/2011).

"Son, be on guard for the enemy is increasing his foul tactics everywhere. He desires to thwart your revival and the renewal of my people. You must warn them not to be deceived. The world is crashing, but I will not be overcome nor will my people if they follow my word. Stay focused on me and my plans. Forget the media who are so variable from day to day. Do not heed the allure of the world. Keep your eyes focused on me.

"I am the savior and I am totally correct for my Father and politically correct for any happening. I assure you that tough times are coming, but will not affect you if you walk with me and stay connected to my word. He who has eyes to see should keep their eyes on me and not on the verbal conflicts happening everywhere" (4/17/2011).

"Son, some have spoken of things being shaken. That is too mild for they should have said things are crashing. How can things be rebuilt unless they crash?

"Look around you and see that everything material or immaterial must be redone in my world. Yes, I will refresh my world, but terrible things will happen first.

"People need a beacon to guide them and to run to. My church is supposed to be that refuge of love and truth. Welcome these new folks with open arms and know that my love will pour forth by my Spirit" *(4/24/2011)*.

"Lord, Independence Day was marvelous with words, songs, music, and fireworks which were truly beautiful. You are to be praised for letting us see your glorious creations. It makes me want more of you, Lord. The book comes along, but there is more to do before the detail work."

"Son, have I not helped you all along? Have I not inspired new chapters recently? Fear not; it is coming together in my name. Don't look aside for you will see distractions. Concentrate on my kingdom where we are friends. I have heard you and will surprise you" (7/5/2011).

"Lord, a good day yesterday; it was good to get out and thanks for the rain."

"Son, all is well in my kingdom. It is yours that is a mess. Listen to my Spirit and let my love flow through you. You are fortunate as very few know or sense my humor. You know I love you. Watch out for snakes dressed as humans. They are not in my will. Keep plugging away; you won't have fears for I am Lord and in control of families, finances, food, and fun. Now relax, my son, and have fun in my kingdom" (7/8/2011).

"A beautiful day, Lord—send even more clouds to paint the sky. I think of you more as a friend. Oh, yes, Lord, a savior, but also a truly wonderful friend-always there-always with a reminder of your love and always with a word of peace."

"Son, things will rapidly accelerate. The earth will rebel against sin itself. There will be much suffering. Now change is come, prophetic change. Nothing will surprise my people, but others will wonder. I have said 'Don't fear' and I mean it. I am in charge of my people. Look to me for guidance in all things. You will need me and I will be there for you. Your family must know a tidal wave is coming, is almost here and will envelop the earth" (7/10/2011).

"Lord, yesterday was wonderful when I looked in church at the verse on the big screen and your Spirit gave me understanding how you see what the Father does. The speaker may have used John 5:19 for something else, but you revealed it was really a veiled Trinitarian meaning."

"Son, you have just scratched the surface. There is so much more to be revealed. Stay open and it will come" *(8/14/2011).*

"Lord, what is going on?'

"Son, you ask what is happening in the world?" It is a living catalog of sin perpetrated by mankind. I once asked, 'Will any faith be found?" You can divide faith into so many sub species. That is the true picture of my church today. Only in the kingdom will you find power, power to change a nation or the world. The power is there, my power, but what is missing is the vision. Man looks to man, not me. Have you ever seen such endless talk that accomplishes nothing? I grow weary listening and watching the frustrations of mankind. Therefore, my glory will soon be evident. Stay tuned, son; you will be amazed" (9/26/2011).

"Son, a lot is going to happen simultaneously. It is going to be here and there so much so that people cannot react nor understand. That is where fear comes in. You know my command so you will be without fear. Not so the masses. Be ready to answer them. Realization-Repentance-Redemption is a good summary" (9/28/2011).

CHAPTER 20

WHAT'S NEXT?

DECISION TIME

The next step is up to you, the reader, and the Holy Spirit. We have talked about the sanctified life and how to get there. We have examined many of the scriptural gifts as well as other gifts people are experiencing. Have you ever wondered what gifts you have? Don't spend too much time thinking as the Holy Spirit will provide just the right gift needed for each situation. The gifts belong to the Holy Spirit and are given to us for ministry through us by Him.

In the narrative of Paul's journey to Rome, Luke shows how a number of gifts operated on the trip.

Wisdom—"Men, I can see that this voyage is bound to meet with disaster and heavy loss, not only to ship and cargo, but to our lives as well" (Acts 27:10).

Discernment—"You should have taken my advice and not sailed from Crete" (Acts 27:21).

Prophecy—"None among you will be lost; only the ship" (Acts 27:22).

Knowledge—"God has granted safety to all who are sailing with you" Acts 27:23-24).

Faith—"I trust that it will all work out just as I have been told" (Acts 27:25).

Prophecy—"Though we still have to face shipwreck on some island" (Acts 27:26).

Discernment—"If these men do not stay with the ship, you have no chance to survive" (Acts 27:31).

Prophecy—"Not one of you shall lose a hair of his head" (Acts 27:34).

Miracle—"This gave new courage, and they too had something to eat" (Acts 27:35-36).

Miracle—"But Paul shook the snake off into the fire and suffered no ill effects from the bite" (Acts 28:5).

Healing—"Paul went in to see the man and praying, laid his hands on him and cured him" (Acts 28:8-9).

These could be examples of the Holy Spirit working in his daily life aboard ship. Paul didn't wonder what gift he should use nor what gifts were operative. He just followed the Holy Spirit's direction. As Christians, we should also be open to his leading and directions. What percentage of God's leading do you think we follow? I know in my case, it was very few in the early walk in the new life. Frankly, I didn't follow most of the promptings. However, God is so patient and loving, he always gave other chances. Eventually, I recognized his voice or leanings and acted accordingly, sometimes.

The one gift that was in operation was tongues. Perhaps, it was the Holy Spirit asking Jesus to be patient with me. Our one gift is the personal prayer language or tongues. This is wonderful and connects us directly to God with a heavenly language that only he understands. It cannot be understood by any of the evil powers. Just imagine: no interruptions while praying and no demonic temptations or put-downs. Also over the years, the Holy Spirit may give other heavenly languages to us as he is flexible as well as loving.

When I was baptized in the Spirit, nothing happened. I didn't feel warmth nor did I receive the gift of tongues. The sage advice I received was, "Cool it; tongues will come." When the gifts came to me it was like a download as I received many of them at the same anointing. Later when I was involved in ministry, it was amazing how the Holy Spirit used his gifts as needed. The right one was just there to help the person. Later I found it fruitful before praying for a person to ask the Holy Spirit how I should pray for the person. It took me a lot of years before I realized this. Previously, I just charged ahead and started praying for them.

As mentioned earlier, the Baptism is usually preceded by water baptism. But God doesn't relate to our schedules, dogmas, or beliefs. One of my favorite passages is narrated in the book of Acts. The Holy Spirit wanted to demonstrate that with the denial of the Messiah by the chosen people, the kingdom was going to be opened to the gentiles. It happened this way: Cornelius, a Roman Centurion had invited Peter to His quarters in Caesarea as the result of an angelic encounter. As Peter related the good news to the Romans, the Holy Spirit was given to them and they began to speak in tongues.

Scripture says the Jewish believers were astounded that the Holy Spirit was given to the gentiles. I can see the Jewish believers totally surprised and saying, "Wait a minute! What's going on here? The Pentecost experience is only for the chosen race! Besides, these foreigners aren't even baptized which has to come first!" Fortunately, Peter realized what had happened and the Romans were baptized. Isn't the Holy Spirit great? We have our rules and procedures, but he is God (Acts 10:1-48).

Tradition usually states that the church was born on Pentecost when the Spirit came on the apostles and disciples. With the advent of Cornelius and his friends, the church was open to the entire world. It wasn't that many years following when Constantine made Christianity the official religion of the Roman Empire.

PART 3
THE GIFTED

Chapter 21

NOT SO GIFTED

A Polite Awakening

The following narration by an unknown author explains what we could miss in our daily Christian walk.

People for People

I was hungry and you formed a humanities club and discussed my hunger. Thank you.

I was imprisoned and you crept off quietly to your chapel and prayed for my release.

I was naked and in your mind you debated the morality of my appearance.

I was sick and you knelt and thanked God for your health.

I was homeless and you preached to me of the spiritual shelter of the love of God.

I was lonely and you left me alone to pray for me.

You seem so holy, so close to God, but I am very lonely, and hungry and cold.

NOT SO GREEN, BUT YELLOW

The narration above shows that not everything is necessarily religiously green with individuals and some churches. The politically correct philosophy of the secular world has imbued the church world. There is a yellow light everywhere that proclaims—caution, caution. It is true; the Body of Christ is fragmented. The social gospel is becoming widespread. Replacement Theology has risen. We can't apply the term full gospel church to all churches, even if they claim to be Christian. The reason is the buffet edition of the bible. This is the pick and choose variety. In other words, parts of the bible are ignored, disbelieved, modified, or enhanced. Such actions are mentioned as a concern in both the Old Testament and the New Testament. "In your observance of the commandments of the Lord, your God, which I enjoin upon you, you shall not add to what I command you nor subtract from it" (Deuteronomy 4:2). "See that you do all I command you; do not add to it or take from it" (Deuteronomy 12:32 NIV).

In the book of Revelation the Spirit says: "I warn everyone who hears the words of prophecy of this book: If anyone adds anything to them, God will add to him the plagues described in this book. And if anyone takes words away from this book of prophecy, God will take away from him his share in the tree of life and in the holy city, which are described in this book" (Revelation 22:18-19 NIV). When it comes to a possibility of changing the word of God, we need to see a red light.

The problem is the denominational issue. The Protestant Revolution solved many problems but opened the way for many more to develop over the years. Christianity should be as easy as Love God; Love your neighbor. The major thrust should be the relationship with Christ and fellow mankind. Instead, it is the adherence to man-made rules. These strong tenets then become arguable beliefs as "My church is better than your church."

God foresaw that such religious actions would happen and had Isaiah prophesize against them: "The Lord says, 'These people come near me with their mouth and honor me with their lips, but their hearts are far from me. Their worship of me is made up only of rules taught by men" (Isaiah 29:13 NIV).

This passage is not just another prophecy in the Old Testament. Jesus actually refers to this passage in two of the gospel narratives: Matthew 15:8-9 and Mark 7:6-7.

CHAPTER 22

TRULY GIFTED

GUESS WHO!

I had considered naming well known gifted Christians and then discuss their attributes and known virtues. However, I realized no matter how many I picked, I would miss some. Besides, I would receive many nominations for people's favorite holy person. I thought I would also receive negative comments of people I had chosen. Therefore, I determined to discuss the truly gifted according to scripture. This is not a list of everyone in the bible, but the winner will surprise you.

One of the most gifted men was John the Baptist. After all, he was sanctified in his mother's womb and led an austere life and prophetically announced the coming of the Messiah. When he saw Jesus for the first time he received a word of knowledge and proclaimed, "Look! There is the Lamb of God who takes away the sin of the world" (John 1:29b).

Clearly, he was a gifted man of influence, but not as potentially important as you, the reader of *Gifted*. Are you surprised at that statement? Don't be for Jesus not only loves you, but also believes in you. He said, "I solemnly assure you, history has not known a man born of woman greater than John the Baptizer, yet the least born into the kingdom of God is greater than he" (Matthew 11:11).

John the Baptist was the last prophet of the old covenant and Jesus the first prophet of the new covenant. Due to the redemption of Jesus and our acceptance of him we become kingdom members.

PART 4

EVER WONDER
WHAT GOD THINKS?

CHAPTER 23

INTRODUCTION TO PROPHECIES

HEAVENLY LESSONS FROM PRAYER GROUPS

I wanted to name Part 4 about what God says. However, I did not want any confusion with the revealed word of prophecies in scripture. Therefore, I used the phrase **What God Thinks**. If you were ever curious about the mind of God, he has surely revealed himself. The bible is a record of God inspiring people to convey his thoughts, precepts, commandments, wrath, and especially his love and forgiveness. In the following chapters, the author is the Holy Spirit. The words or thoughts by the Holy Spirit are given through blessed people. You won't find any prophecies from the nationally known prophetic people, just ordinary Spirit-filled Christians. My only work was typing which of the many modern prophecies I thought would be interesting.

The word prophecy is commonly accepted as pertaining to the future. However, in the spiritual life, prophetic words are sometimes meant for the present moment or for the future. God created mankind wanting to share his love and longs for us to return. Therefore, throughout History he has communicated either in person or through his prophets.

The early prophets spoke mainly of the coming Messiah to the Jewish people. Jesus fulfilled those prophecies and spoke many more prophecies to guide us. This is confirmed in scriptures which said, "In times past, God spoke in fragmentary and varied ways to our fathers through the prophets; in this final age, he has spoken to us through his Son whom he has made heir of all things and through whom he first created the universe" (Hebrews 1:1-2).

Ever since the church was created at Pentecost, God has sent his Holy Spirit to dwell within us. The wonderful result is that each Spirit-filled Christian can function at times with the gift of prophecy as well as any of the other gifts of the Spirit. Paul talks about this wonderful gift in the 13th chapter of Corinthians. "Set you hearts on spiritual gifts—above all, the gift of prophecy" (1 Corinthians 13:1a).

This part of the book is about prophecy, the gift of divinely ordained words spoken by God's servants. You may wonder if prophecy is or was necessary. God thought so and told us, "I will raise up for them a prophet like you from among their kinsmen, and will put my words into his mouth; he shall tell them all that I command him" (Deuteronomy 18:18). These words were spoken to Moses and portions of this work were quoted by Jesus during His temptation.

The first prophets usually recognized are Amos and Hosea who were risen up to say something new preceded by the attention-getting words, "Thus saith the Lord." Throughout the Old Testament, there were prophets noted historically as major and minor ones. The distinction was made on the length of the word, not on the content. Clearly, Moses, Isaiah, Jeremiah, Daniel, and Ezekiel, are the most well-known names of prophets.

While there are famous prophets of the Old Testament, clearly, Jesus is the main prophet of the New Testament. But Jesus not only fulfilled many of the prophecies of the Old Testament and said so, he prophesied about the future. In addition, many of the writers of the New Testament were prophets as well. Had the world studied these

New Testament prophecies, we would not be in an international crisis as they are unfolding just as they were written and predicted thousands of years ago.

St. Paul explains that this gift is for the church, not the prophet. St. Paul also states that we should eagerly seek love which is the first commandment and the spiritual gifts and especially the gift of Prophecy (1 Cor.14:1).

The question is what was the bridge between the prophets of the Old and the New Testament? The prophets of old were few in number compared to the throngs of Jewish people, but were ordained by God as a ministry. In the New Testament, Jesus came to fulfill the Law and renewed the ministry of prophecy which had fallen aside among the Jewish people. For the followers of Jesus, the bridge was the day of Pentecost when the gifts of the Holy Spirit were poured forth on the church. One of these gifts was prophecy (1 Cor.12:10). The difference in the testaments is the availability of the prophetic gift. While the ministry of the gift of prophecy is inherent in both testaments, due to Pentecost, anyone who is Spirit-filled may be used by our Lord to proclaim his word in prophecy.

Formerly known as the *Book of Wisdom*, the book of *Proverbs* explained the reason for the gift of prophecy as, "Without prophecy, the people become demoralized, but happy is he who keeps the law" (Proverbs 29:18). Is prophecy for our day? Sir Isaac Newton thought so when he described what is actually happening in the twenty-first century: "About the time of the end, a body of men will be raised up who will turn their attention to the prophecies, in the midst of much clamor and confusion." This refers not only to the modern focus on ancient biblical prophecies, but also to the numerous prophetic words being spoken in our time.

In 20111 and 2012, there are numerous recognized prophets speaking at conferences. Some even have their own web sites where you can review how the Lord is using them. However, the Lord also speaks to people in gatherings to proclaim his love in a prophetic way. These people may be used occasionally in this manner, but they would not be considered as full time prophetic ministers.

I was affiliated with charismatic prayer groups starting in the 1970's and kept a record of how God uses his people, regardless of gender, denomination, race, or age to speak his word. Many times he gave the same or similar words to one or more people. After a prophecy was given and someone said "I can confirm that," there was an inaudible but nevertheless real inner sigh by the one who gave the prophecy. The week before I wrote this, I received an e-mail saying exactly this, namely confirming a prophecy the Lord had me give recently. If we were complete and so perfectly trusting, we wouldn't need such confirmation. But Jesus knows our weakness and is so compassionate that this confirmation builds up our confidence and hope in him.

Next, we'll examine prophecies from the 20th and 21st Century. Actually, for this work I've sifted through numerous prophecies from 1976 through 2012. These prophecies over time show some of his thoughts and how he responded to the times. These words are from the Holy Spirit as the author but they were given by finite human beings. They were spoken across the country and show his guidance and his corrections as well as his love. The prophecies were tested as authentic by local leaders at the time they were given. They were spoken at prayer groups, church services, conferences, and leader's meetings. In some, God is talking to a group; in others, to elders; in others, to the pastors or prayer group leaders, but always as a friend and lover. Some of these are very inspirational; hopefully they can lead you to further meditation. Rather than commenting on each year, I hope you will concentrate on God's words and see how they touch you. I suggest you just read a few prophecies and then spend time with the Holy Spirit.

With any non-biblical prophecy, discernment must be used to ascertain the validity of the words spoken. If a particular prophecy doesn't touch you, move on. Paul stated, "Do not stifle the Spirit. Do not despise prophecies. Test everything; retain what is good" (1 Thessalonians 5:19-20).

We are going to start with prophecies given a prayer group in Detroit, Michigan that started in a living room in 1972 with three people. As they began to grow in numbers, they experienced personnel problems and some folks left the group. As they grew larger and larger they moved to a school room and finally to the church hall. The group then expanded into separate prayer groups in three different churches.

At the 1976 Pentecost Mass, Cardinal Deardon called for the Detroit Charismatic Renewal Groups to form stronger groups. This original group grew to about 250 people. While it was held in a Catholic parish, the people were from numerous denominations.

Chapter 24

1976

"You are now coming on a new age. I have chosen you and I have chosen you for a mighty work. This work lies ahead. You are to be a witness here to this community as I am forming you and strengthening you. I want to do mighty things here with you. Be open" (7/21/76).

"Don't be afraid to listen to your heart. My words are not that hard to understand. Beware of those who call themselves Christian, but do not follow me or my Son, Jesus. Beware of any sect that puts some other man in my place. Follow me; read my word. I speak to you. My glory will shine before you. Do not be afraid; I will come in glory" (8/4/76).

COMMENTARY:

The heavenly Father seems to gather His people within his arms and warns them of roving wolves. He is saying that just because a person goes to church every week, that doesn't make them a Christian. Nor does a person calling themselves a Christian automatically guarantee this. Christianity is the result of accepting Jesus as Savior and asking forgiveness for our sins. This is confirmed in scripture as being born again.

"I come to you tonight with a stern message. You have held back too long. You must come out of yourselves now. It is time to draw close to one another. I am instructing you to do this. Do not be afraid of one another for I have given you that name-that name for love. I call you to love now" (8/4/76).

COMMENTARY:

This group wasn't actively close to one another. It was like attending a meeting where only a few people knew each other and the others were strangers.

"I call you to a deep commitment; I call you to trust one another, but first of all, know one another. Don't put this off. Be committed" (8/11/76).

COMMENTARY:

This prophecy is like the previous one. God repeats His request that the people should learn to know each other. Afterward, He requires trust.

"I want you to listen-listen carefully. I have been instructing you for some time to get to know one another. I want you to take action. I want you to act on this. I want you to know your brother and sister in the Lord" (9/1/76).

"I am building in this community; I am building something very strong. Each of you only looks like stones now, but each of you must depend on one another. Each of you must have this cement. Each of you must have this bond of oneness. You can only look to me for this oneness. This is your tie. This tie is the tie of the love of the Lord. This is what I ask of you. Just to love; just to let love overflow; just to give of yourselves. Give of yourselves because you love me" (10/13/76).

"I am the light. I am the light sometimes far away, but I never go away. I am coming to show you the light in all its brilliance. Be patient. I am doing things you cannot understand. I am molding; I am shaping. Each of you now has gone through this process. I tried to build something strong. I have been building; now you must act. You must act upon your strength. I call you to these deeper walks. I will no longer emphasize this" (12/1/76).

"I am calling you and going to give direction. You have been purified and now I am calling you to something new again. I am calling you to put aside these things, these burdens. I am calling you now to walk the walk of joy. Though these times seem hard, this is what I am going to ask of you. I am going to ask for that joy; I want other people to see that joy in you; this is a command. This must be done. Put those things aside for now—let us see that joy; remember I have given you everything" (12/8/76).

"In this New Year you are going to see wonderful miracles happen. In this New Year many people in your family are going to come to know me. I am using each of you and I expect to do great things by using you as instruments. This is what you are. Now you must reflect my glory. Now people must see me through you. The time is over for you to carry your burdens. In this New Year I ask that you show your joy. I ask that people see your love—my love for you. I ask that you do these things for me. Yes, you will have problems, but I ask you to take them to me. I ask you not to dwell on them. I ask you to let me work with you in all situations for you are going to see miracles" (12/22/76).

"In this New Year, I am going to want you to follow my instructions carefully for you are to rely totally on me for direction. And there are things that I am going to ask of you. Your hearts are to be prepared. You are to be open and ready to be used. I have taken you through a process. This process for many will last a long time, but for others I would like you to be open. So many people out there do not know me, and I am going to ask you to show them my love. You must also love one another; you must break down those barriers that are holding you apart; melt those barriers; do what you have to do to bring yourselves closer to one another. You are going to need this strength for in this New Year I am going to call you to greater things. I am going to call my people here and I expect you will be able to give to these people. For the time is coming to give back. This is what I'm asking: give back and show that abundant love that I have given you" (12/29/77).

CHAPTER 25

GROWTH

"I am calling you now to a new direction and in that direction I am going to ask for a deeper devotion, for a deeper commitment to me. In this new direction, you are to become very close to me. You are not to waste your time as you have in the past for you are to call on me for everything. I am going to ask that you deepen your love for one another and from this I'm going to call many people. Many people need this love and I want to pour this love out. You will have to be my instruments. You must deepen yourselves; you must become close to me, closer than before" (1/5/77).

"I am calling you now to repentance for I want to make you whole. In order to be whole, you must drop these things at my feet. You must look at the cross for I bore your sins. You are not to harbor these things anymore. You are to look deep into yourselves now. Look to those areas. Do not put them aside any longer for I want to clean and purify you. You are to be made whole for you are to be my servants. I'm going to expect that you really look to yourselves and bring these things before me" (1/19/77).

COMMENTARY:

A new season brings growth but with the need to discard the many personal crosses each of us carry.

"You are in my heart. Come follow me, I will show you the way. Do not walk too fast for you will only stumble. Don't be afraid for I will guide you in my wisdom. Take little steps and make them firm and secure so that they may re-enforce the next ones. I am leading you gently as only I can. You may think you are small, but you are an intricate and essential part of my eternal plan that only I know. Do not be led astray by others. "Follow the leadings of my Spirit, for you know him. My plan for you is different than for all others. You are to grow and blossom as flowers, all different, but still flowers giving forth different fruit, but all for my glory. Do not say I wish I were a rose or a tulip, but know yourselves and grow in what I have given you. You together have a job in my great plan. Follow my lead and with all I give, you will know my will, for I love you and will share good things with you forever if only you follow me in love. Hear my words and rejoice for I am the Lord God of hosts and power" (2/5/77).

"My Dearest children, I call you together to sing my praises, my glory; to sing of my gentleness and my tenderness with you; to sing of my forgiveness of your faults and sins; they are as no more. I delight in you, in your coming before me to praise me and sing to me" (2/5/77).

"Heed my voice on the following things: I'm asking you again for that deep commitment that I've been asking for quite some time, but many of you are not following my ways on this. I've been asking you to put aside those things that are drawing you away from me. I've been calling you now to obedience for I am going to show you the fruit in your life. Yes, the fruit of love is what I would like to see. You are to really see this love outpour to people. You are to see healings through this love. You are to see miracles happening. But you are putting your own stumbling block in the way. Where are your gods now? Take a look in your life: what are your gods? What are you placing before me? Look to these and remove those things instantly.

"You are not to belabor this point. You are to put me first and all else behind. I'm calling you now as an army, and I've been calling you for something. But an army needs strength. Without me first, you will have no strength; you will have no blessings because I have to be first in your life. All the rest must be put aside now. Then you will see the blessings flow in your life because I am your God. My children, no other things should be put before me" (2/7/77).

"You have only begun to see my glory because I am so willing to pour out these things to you. I am so willing to love you, but you must let go of all those things that hold you back. Look to me only; take away all those gods in your lives; take yourself out of so many situations and just look at me for I want your life to be totally built and centered around me and I want you to have that great faith. I want you to be my chosen people. I want to bless you abundantly. Just trust in that tremendous love I have for you and let me work these situations out. Just pray that you step aside; just trust" (2/8/77).

"I give you a command now that you must stop putting feet in both worlds. You must commit yourself now to one or the other. You must make your choice: You either commit yourself to me: to live that life to the fullest with no holding back or you commit yourself to the world. This is your choice. I allow you to have that choice freely, but I'm there as a loving Father. I'm there with arms wide open, but I want those hearts of yours and I want you to be sincere. Stop trying to thread the needle of two worlds. Make your choice" (2/9/77).

"There is a forest of green grass. I'm calling you to come out of the desert; come out and sit with me. Come sit with me in the green and refreshing forest. Come and rest your spirits; I will give you living water. I will refresh you. Fountains of water will spring up within you. Come out of the desert; come to me as I'm waiting for you. Come and rest with me and I will show you the love I have for you. Open your hearts and find rest in me" (2/10/77).

"I come to you tonight asking you to let my word into your life. Let me fight these battles that are yours. It saddens me when you try to fight them yourself. Turn to me and I will deliver you. I will deliver you like I delivered my people, Israel. Turn to me and I will guide you and set you free.

"I love you; I want you to know that but I call you to be disciples and you do nothing. I call you to go forth as disciples and you do nothing. Time grows short and I want you to go forth in the power of my Spirit. I have many things I need to accomplish through you. I need you to do my will. I want you to hear me. Hear my voice and act on it. You are not to worry; you are only to listen to me. To hear me is to know my will. To know my will is to be one with me" (2/11/ 1977).

"I call you my children because you are indeed my children. I call you to be my children, but I do not call you to be children. I call you to be adults. I call you to maturity. I now call you my people. My people are maturing until they finally grow to full adults. By this I mean to be as children to trust me completely as your children trust you. But you as loving mothers and fathers expect your children to grow to adulthood. And so to my children, I trust that you will grow to adulthood. Don't be afraid to grow. Don't be afraid to step out of your childhood into adulthood. This is the proper order of things. Don't be afraid of the adulthood I'm calling you to" (2/12/77).

"Do not look far ahead of me and try to walk too far ahead of me. Remember, I am calling you to daily growth and daily devotion. Do not try to look through a tunnel to the future to where the doors are open or what I am leading you to. Try to go day by day and to follow what I am teaching you daily and to put this into effect.

In this way you will grow as Christians. In this way you will grow closer to me. Do not look too much to the future. Look to the now. Look to where you need to improve now. This is what I would have you learn" (2/13/77).

"Every week I call you my people. Know that I, your God, have chosen you; you have not chosen me. And since I have chosen you, I can call you my people. Know also that I have the storehouse; I have the wealth; I have the abundance; I have all the things that are for my people. Come to me and let me do it; let me help you; let me give you what I have as a Father" (2/14/77).

"My children, heed my words now. You are my disciples and unless you are hearing my voice daily, you will not know what course I will have you on. I want you now, day by day, to ask me where you should be that day; to ask me who it is you should talk to. I want this simplicity and I want you to obey and follow through because this is the only way you can truly be disciples of mine" (2/16/77).

"I showed you my love tonight. I ask you now, when you leave this place, don't go back to the way you were when you walked in. Look to me. Just keep your eyes on me and I promise I will walk with you and guide you with your problems" (2/16/77).

"I am glad that you came to me. It fills my heart when you come to me. I love you, my children. Tonight, you give me great joy, great pleasure. Tonight come to me; ask anything you would have me do for you. Just turn to me tonight" (2/17/77).

"Now as never before you will need to trust me. I am calling you to a new awakening of my presence in your midst. I call you to submit yourselves wholly and completely to my directions, not shrinking from trials and crosses, but offering everything up out of love for me. My children, you cannot grow; your spirit cannot be truly free until you learn to look at all these things as steps to come nearer to me. Fear not my hand of correction on you. It is a loving Father who does this. Trust me; trust me for my love is unending; I call you in love" (3/18/77).

CHAPTER 26

MATURITY

"I wish to surround you tonight with my comfort, my peace, and my joy. All those who hear my voice, come and follow me; turn to me; look to me. I have prepared a way for you and it leads to eternal glory. I am preparing a place for you. Do not fear; just reach out for my hand. In times of need I am there. I am walking that road with you. I never leave your side. This place of glory is with me and I'm calling all of you there tonight to give me yourself, give me your heart. That is what I ask of you to do and then I ask you to listen to my word. Obey my commandments; do the things I've asked you to do; the things I say in my word. That is how I call you to my word and I say, 'Follow Me.' It is a place of glory that I am preparing for you and tonight I surround you with my love. My children, be at peace in your heart" (2/18/77).

"My word I lay upon your heart. Preach my word by your love, by who you are and by your closeness with me. Preach it not in words that are empty. Be not as sounding brass or a tinkling cymbal, but be a living breathing person of love with one hand in mine and one hand in the hand that you take care of" (9/7/77).

"I call you to unity. I call you to be one in the Spirit, one in mind. I set before you, my son, Jesus. I call you to be an army, a discipled people. I will humble you that you may become disciplined, that you might submit to my will. You do not know what I have in store for you. If you only knew, if you could hear my word and see my plan. I call you from your ways of the flesh to the ways of my Spirit, to ways of new life and strength.

This is my word to you that you would come to me; come to me and know me. I have much love for you. I seek to unite you. Come to me each day. I call you to be one in unity. I call you to be gathered to fellowship with one another, to grow in my love, for you have Jesus as a common bond. Put on my spirit and grow" (7/78).

"I give you your feet that you might walk and be with my people. I give you your hands that you might serve me. I give you your mouth that you might praise me and share me with others. I give you your eyes that my light might shine through them. And I give you my heart, my heart that is in you that you may grow more and more like me" (7/78).

"You have heard my word this night. You have heard the facts. Now I ask you to put your faith in that word. Walk through the dark valleys; walk around the trees, through any obstacles that might come in your pathways. And when you have done that you will come into the area of feelings; you will be there; you will be in the light. You'll experience me and you will know my presence in ways that you have never known me before" (7/78).

Chapter 27

SECURING GROWTH

"You are my creation. I have called you before I even made the world; I have called you to come to me. I tell you now to walk with me; I will walk with you and you will feel my love" (3/77).

"You are in my heart. Come follow me. I will show you the way. Do not walk too fast for you will only stumble. Don't be afraid for I will guide you in my wisdom. Take little steps and make them firm and secure so that they may reinforce the next ones. I am leading you gently as only I can.

"You may think you are small, but you are an intricate and essential part of my eternal plan that only I know. Do not be led astray by others. Follow the leadings of my Spirit for you know him. My plan for you is different than for others. You are to grow and bloom as flowers, all different, but still flowers giving forth different fruit, but all for my glory.

"Do not say I wish I were a rose or a tulip, but know yourselves and grow in what I have given you for you together have a job in my great plan. Follow my lead with all I give you and know my will. For I love you and will share good things with you forever if you only follow me in love. Hear my words and rejoice for I am the

Lord God of Hosts and Power. I have come into your midst. Listen; believe and obey" (3//77).

"Hold on to your fears no longer because I'm calling you to put aside all these barriers now and to start trusting. Remember, you can no longer be in two worlds. You must dedicate yourself to me and trust me fully in everything I do. You are called to dedicate yourselves deeper now, each and every one of you. Look to me and trust in everything I am doing" (4/77).

"I have been preparing you like an army. You have been in training. You have been like vessels that have been spotted. I am trying to wipe those blemishes away, yet you cling on to those things that are to be dead now. You must be purified because you will need my strength.

"Many of you will fall to the wayside. There will only be a remnant, a true remnant left to sing my praises. Things will not be easy. You are clinging to the world, but there will be no security there for many things are going to be swept away. Things will be difficult; prepare yourselves now. Prepare yourselves by getting closer to me. Prepare yourselves be freeing yourselves. Do not cling to the vanities of the world. Be free; keep your eyes straight. Direct yourself upon me and the goals of the kingdom for all else will not bring you security. All else will fall to the wayside.

"Do not be afraid; I will always be with you. Even though things may look the darkest, look to the sunshine and look to that relationship with me. But begin training and begin now" (12/7/77).

"I see where you are, but I also know where you are going and what you will become. While at times there may be confusion and you wonder what is going on, nevertheless, know this, that I am leading you and am also drawing the prayer group. I know what you will become and it will be done. You will accomplish what I have in mind" (1977).

CHAPTER 28

CORE GROUP GUIDELINES

"I am calling you to a new direction. I am going to use you as a catalyst. I want you to make a deeper commitment to each other. There will be many problems in the years ahead, but I will be there. Just look to me" (12/20/76).

"I am calling you to go forth now; I am calling you to be like apostles and in this, I'm going to want you to help gather my people. I am calling you to be leaders; I am calling you to be shepherds. I am calling you to a greater dedication. I am calling you closer to me" (1/3/77).

"There will be many difficult times, but remember, I am going to be there. You cannot see the future, but be close to me. There are so many things that I have planned for you. Be open to my Spirit. Ask ме where you should be" (1/3/77).

"Now you are only seeing a part of the picture for I am unfolding some of my glory to you. You are looking through blinders now. My glory is so great that I am exposing little by little to you. I have told you to expect miracles. This is what I am telling you. You are going to see many people come to the Lord this year. You are going to see miracles happen; expect this to happen. I am pouring forth my Spirit to people and I expect you to show that great joy, and that love and be excited; be happy during these times. This is what I'm asking you because I am the miracle worker and I am showing my glory now" (2/14/77).

"I see where you are; I know where you are and I am drawing you toward me one step at a time. Look to me, but don't run toward me because you go beyond my time. Walk slowly in my spirit and as you keep your eyes on me; you will be on the path. You won't veer to the right or veer to the left, but you will come straight toward me. Know that I am drawing you towards me and you will be met" (2/14/77).

"Be shepherds and draw people to you by your love like I would draw them. This is what I am calling you to. Encircle My people now with love for this is what we desperately need" (2/14/77).

"I called you here today because I want you to fully realize that within your spirit is the power of healing. You have not called on

127

this power of healing in the Spirit and it is workable. And I call you to faith in my word. You have been remiss in this area, my children, and this is why I called you tonight, to bring this knowledge to you." (1977).

"My Spirit proclaims healing and my Spirit dwells in each of you and I call you tonight to proclaim this healing to others, to bring my healing to others. You are leaving my children in sickness. You are leaving them with broken spirits because you are not proclaiming this gift that I have given you, this power that is within you. It is my power; it is your power through me. Keep this in mind. Use what I have given you. My love gift is healing to my people. This is as great a gift to them as the love that I bear them. Do you understand" (3/20/78)?

"Do not depend upon your own understanding; only depend on my word. If you lean upon your own understanding, you will look for answers and you will not find them. No, you cannot lean on your understanding. You must pray with the power of my Spirit. This is what I ask of you. Believe in my promises. They are truth" (3/20/78).

CHAPTER 29

PASTORAL GUIDELINES

"Don't listen and think, 'I'm not a disciple' for you are truly disciples. I have called you to discipleship now. It's time to face the fact that you are disciples. You are the ones I've called out of the people. You are the ones I depend on.

"I've given you authority; I've given you insight; I've given you leadership. But maybe it's a discipleship right now that you haven't considered. Think about it for a moment in terms of one another. So many times you thought about one another as: 'How can I help you; what can I do for you, sister or brother'" (2007)?

"How can you grow in love? You can all learn from each other. It's a resource you haven't looked to before; you have overlooked it. There's so much richness in each of you, so much tenderness, so much love that I have poured out in each one. I want you as you grow in discipleship to learn the true meaning of discipleship. You have the resources that I have placed in each one of you. Learn and grow from one another; love one another; you are my body. Each part depends on the other part to sustain itself, to maintain itself to be whole. I am your head; you are my body; you are my disciples. See me in each one of you" (1977).

"You are like flowers in a garden. The colors you see are the fruits and gifts I pour forth on you. The scents you smell are my love for you. My people, I wish to use you to draw the people to me. Let them see that love, peace, and joy that you reflect as a flower reflects my love. Let them see that underneath in you. For they will see me in you" (1977).

"What is it you have? I want to use you. You are my people; I will use you. My dear, beloved children, can you look at one another and see me? Can you do this thing for me? But you cannot seek to find out why. I ask you to bear-up with one another's faults and weaknesses as I bear up with your faults and weaknesses.

"I ask that you truly love one another as I love you. This is why I call you together, to secure that bond of love. I want you to be close together. I want you to be one mind, one heart: my mind, my heart. That's what I ask of you. Can you do this for me? Truly love one another. Remaining in my love is my joy. Give me that joy, my people." (1977).

"Greater love has no man than to lay down his life for his brother. I ask you to lay down your lives for your brother. You have your way and your brother has his way. I ask you both to lay down your ways and seek my way. The Spirit of truth will lead you" (1977).

"I will take all of you children; follow me along the road. I cannot promise it will be all sunshine; you will be burdened and the road will be darkened, but lay down your burdens to one another. Lay them in my outstretched arms to embrace you.

"This is pure joy when faith is tested. Realize that when the faith is tested this makes for endurance and when endurance comes to its perfection, you will be fully mature and lacking nothing" (1977).

"Get ready for I am sending my Spirit upon you in power. You have all walked with me these years. You've walked with me and you have learned from me. I have taught you, and now I am ready to send my Spirit upon you in power and you will be my witnesses to the ends of the earth" (5/8/78).

"I said I have been preparing you for a long time now; I have been preparing all of my people all over the world for the coming of my Spirit in power. Say how should you wait? You have been waiting; you are waiting in trust. Open your heart and expect that Spirit of power to come upon you. You have learned many things and you have learned to trust in me. Sometimes you have felt my presence and sometimes you have not; but you have held firm to that faith that I have given you. And now I say, count on that. Believe those words that I gave you. Stand firm and wait upon my Spirit and it will come in power upon you" (5/8/78).

COMMENTARY BY THE PERSON WHO PROPHESIZED ABOVE:

"This is not a word we are supposed to wait for. It's a *power* that we are supposed to await, a power beyond ourselves. We've stepped out in faith, but the faith has been our faith in Jesus and his word and the faith he has put in our hearts. But what he is telling us is to wait for is a power that is beyond doubt, a power that will give us a strength and courage beyond our comprehension.

The sense of the power that our Lord wants to give us is beyond words—I can't put it into words. I have a sense of such tremendous power beyond anything we've ever known before that I can't find any words to express it. It has nothing to do with the gifts. **We already have the gifts**.

"I do not deal with you about your sins; I deal with you in your relationship with Jesus" (1977).

"I have already blessed you three beyond your dreams. I said I was raising up three leaders beyond yourselves for you thought of leaders in one way, but with me, I had my understanding and my way.

"Unite now and evermore in my love and the love for your brothers and sisters. Go forth boldly, but in obedience. Stand firm to the word I have placed in your hearts this weekend. Be bold; be strong and lead all my people including my leaders. Know that I have chosen you and fear not; my will be done" (1978).

CHAPTER 30

OTHER GROUPS

"Listen to the voice with which I call you. I am calling you to a special awareness of my presence, to a new horizon of life with me. The cost will be your willingness to lay down your entire lives for me. The problems, temptations, and crosses I allow in your lives may seem like you are in darkness for a while, but I do this in order for you to be molded in a more perfect image of me. Do not fear my corrections on you for I love you and will be with you always. You must die to self in order to rise with me in a true resurrection of spirit. Love me totally, holding nothing back. Know that I am with you always" (1977).

"I have spoken in days past and called you my vanguard. Are you listening, discerning, and awaiting my commands? I tell you time grows short. A time of great shaking is fast approaching. Structures standing now will be no more. Conveniences and comforts will cease to exist. My people will exist only by trusting me.

"You are my vanguard. I have called you; I have taught you my word. I have shared my thoughts in the prophetic word. I have used the experiences of your daily life to teach you about my place in your life. If you are my vanguard, my front line troops, are you ready?

If I cannot count on you, whom will I count on? My anointing will rest on you. Will you be able to appropriate it; do you have impediments to doing my will, my command? Does anything stand in your way? Repent! Time is short.

"Many will come to you seeking understanding. Many will come to you wanting to know how to repent. Many will come wondering how you can retain peace in the midst of such conflict and chaos. My people will be wounded deeply and will be seeking healing. You must be equipped. Half measures will not be sufficient for what lies ahead. Come deeper into my heart. Fear is useless. Trust is imperative" (4/27/06).

COMMENTARY:

This prophecy was spoken to a Christian group in 2006 and truly reflects the happenings in 2012 when this is being typed.

"Come now my children, the hour is at hand to separate the wheat from the weeds! It is time for true devotion to be made manifest and bear fruit that will endure and give glory to God.

"What has been tolerated will no longer be tolerated: the lukewarm Christians so called 'do-gooders' who serve their own interests. This is a mockery to true service and sacrificial love" (2007).

"You cannot serve two masters. To hold onto your ambitions and dreams, your many possessions and goals to succeed in this world is folly. The financial world is toppling. Many institutions are crashing and remedies such as politics and advisors cannot fix the rot from within. The lack of love for almighty God and his commandments is the problem. Are you my children totally with me or of the world" (2007)?

CONFIRMATION:

"If you keep my commandments, you will remain in my love, just as I have kept my Father's commandments and remain in his love. I have told you this so my joy might be in you and your joy might be complete" (John 15:9-11).

"Listen to me. Turn off the outside noises that surround you and focus on me. I am your everlasting Lord, the Alpha and Omega. You each belong to me. Hold fast to the truth you know but be open to grow, to expand to become more like me." (2007)

"I gently call you to come. Humbly sit in my presence and learn of my love for you individually and collectively. Let your banner be all inclusive, inviting all into the banquet of love. Come; do not tarry. I have so much that needs to be accomplished through you but with me and because of me." (2007)

"Come in prayer and fasting. Listen. Be open. Be filled with holy boldness and let my truths resound in your hearts as I lead you to holiness and wholeness in my spirit of love and peace. Your group needs to grow. Fertilize it with my Spirit; water it with my love. I planted the seeds long ago but something is missing. Come before me and let me reveal to you what must be done so your group will grow and flourish. Be still. Quiet yourself down and listen to my truth. My truth will set you free. It will undo the bonds that hold you to the past. Rise up! Live! Love! Carry my banner of unending love for all." (2007)

"My people, it is time to let the trumpet sound and show my people what they need. It is time to let the trumpet sound and to lead my people to me and not to the world. The love I have for my people will shine through you. It is time to let the trumpet sound and spread my word. I cherish you. I call you to come before me open and fully surrendered. I call you to cherish me." (2009)

"Listen, Listen, Listen. Time is short. Go back to your roots. What did I ask of you? I asked you to assist me in redeeming my people in your work places, in the market square. But first you must surrender yourself to my love, becoming trusting little children. Only in your own redemption can you be an instrument for my use.

"You are my leaders. I see many adults, but few children in your beloved group. Lead your brothers and sisters in becoming little children. I need trusting little children" (1/26/10).

COMMENTARY:

He is asking us to be dependent, trusting, submissive children to our heavenly Father.

"If you are in the desert place, then you are where I want you to be. In the desert you will be stripped of all you have come to rely on outside of me. What you have come to rely on-your gifts, accomplishments, strengths, professional successes, these are all transitory. It is I who uphold you. It is I who carry you. You can do nothing outside of my grace and providence, not one thing! Who you are is not what you accomplish. Who you are is mine, my little child. Do not fear" (2/2/10).

"I am with you to deliver you. Open your heart to receive my word. Listen attentively for I have much to say. I love you with an everlasting love. I have commissioned you to do a great mission for my kingdom to be all inclusive in whom you invite.

"I have called you to call others into my bosom of love. Listen to their stories and make them your own. Be on guard against the snares of the evil one. Put on the full armor of Christ at all times. Be prepared for battle, a spiritual battle against the principalities and powers of darkness. Unite yourself to me. Be so absorbed in my word that you know my voice. My truth will always set you free. Fine tune your discernment and be attentive to me. I have so much to say. Listen with your whole being and then act upon my word. Be people of action, love, and truth" (2/3/10).

"Look up. Raise your eyes and look about you. What do you see? What do you hear? My people perish for lack of knowledge. My people are suffering. They are in need of your help. Come and be renewed by my holy presence; be filled with my love as you go to those in need, uniting yourself to their pain and renewing and strengthening them in my love.

"Come to me as little children, humble, expectant, full of anticipation, hope and my love that I pour our upon all my children. Open your hearts and let my healing love be poured out on all you meet professionally and socially. Do not keep for yourself the riches I have so lavishly given to you. Be givers and servers of my word, my love, my all. Be united to me" (2/4/10).

Chapter 31

1979 PROPHETIC SUMMARY

The main themes heard over and over were:

1). **<u>Be Open.</u>** Allow Him to work. Allow him to love us. Jesus says, **"Let Me"** as if he is asking for permission. He will not violate our free will. We have a choice which is to follow him or not; to believe or not; to trust or not; to accept or not; to receive or not. We must consciously make that choice.

2). **<u>Repent and Forgive. Bind Together in Love.</u>** These two are so tied together, they cannot be separated. As we are open to Jesus, he heals us. He shows us the need for repentance which he helps us to take care of. He shows us the need for forgiveness.

"As he helps us in these areas, we find ourselves becoming more loving people. We begin to truly see Jesus in our brothers and sisters. We begin to really become one with Jesus and recognize our own uniqueness in the Body of Christ. This is what Jesus means when he says he wants our wholeness. He wants to become Lord of our Lives".

3). **<u>Go Forward-Be My Disciples</u>**. As he heals us and feeds us, we must go and be food for others. We must love them and pray for them, touch them and allow Jesus to heal them: not only allow it, but want it.

CHAPTER 32

THE EIGHTIES

"This year I want you to lean on me more than you ever have. Rely less on your own self, but on my strength. Come to me and know my strength and my power to resist evil as I pour forth my Spirit. How many times have I told you I love you? Know my love; experience my gifts. Reach out; be my hands; be my feet; be my eyes for you are mine and I love you. I wish to form a strong healthy body that cannot be shaken by the wind" (1/7/81).

"Suffering is to kill the weeds that are choking the words, the words that I have brought you. These weeds are the things that have stayed with you from before your life with me. They must die. They must let go and henceforth this causes suffering. I said, 'All of my children must pick up their cross and follow me. I don't say carry it; I say at times to be nailed to it. I am asking you to suffer. Some of you have already; some of you are; some of you will. But come to me in joy and gladness. Know that I love you; know that I am with you and will never leave you.

"You know that my words say, 'My yoke is sweet, my burden is light.' Why are you fearful? Have I not touched you? Fear not! Be at peace! Know my love, my joy, my gift to you. Do not be afraid to suffer. Trust me for I am indeed trustworthy'" (1/14/81).

"Look at me in all you do. My peace and serenity shall see you through. My peace can lead you through daily tasks. Look to me is what I ask. And what is this peace as all falls apart? It is the presence of me living in your heart" (1/21/81).

"Look at me as a suffering servant for that is what I am. And what I am, I ask of you. Come to me and I will give you the strength you need as my Father gave me the strength I needed to be in his will" (1/28/81).

"Know that I am always with you. As you walk in the dark valley, know that I am right by your side. Take my hand and I will lead you, but you must go through that valley. I am the way to the light and I am with you at all times" (1981).

"Truly, I call you my brothers. As Paul said in Hebrews, 'We are of the same stock.' As my Father did, as it was his purpose to bring a great number of his sons into glory. It was appropriate that God, on whom everything exists, should make the leader who would take them to salvation perfect through suffering. For the one who sanctifies and the ones who are sanctified are of the same stock. That is why he openly called them brothers.

"I came to this earth and I suffered to be more like you so that I could atone for your sins. Now I say you must suffer to become more like me to lose some of this earthly dross so you can walk with me more fully and teach others about me and all this comes as one word: love" (1/28/81).

"What did you do with the last word I gave you? You know what I have called you to do. Suffer as I have suffered. Love as I have loved. Heal as I have healed. Be as I am. Do not try to do this on your own. I will give you the strength to do it. Come to me. I *will* give you the strength" (2/25/81).

"Be on your guard. Be steadfast in faith. Resist the enemy's temptations as he tries to take you away from me. All that I have is yours, but you must ask and accept it.

"Use my power that is within you to be a spokesman for me. Do not look at the faults of you brothers and sisters and what you can change. Tell them of your great love for me, that I have filled you with a mighty Spirit; that I am present within you. Help and love them. You need each other.

"I allow situations to come up that would make you angry and frustrated because that is my way of salting you. That allows you a chance to let my light shine" (1981).

"I was slain so that I might become bread, bread for all of you who hunger. Eat of this bread. It will bring you peace and strength and courage. I bind you together to enjoy and to live in me, praising me in all your days. Draw near for I am the fire that burns and purifies you and creates love within you and among you. Do not be afraid. I give the breath of life to each of you. I blow with my wind and I separate the chaff from the wheat" (3/26/86).

"Come and die with me that you might rise to new life. That is my word and it is going to bear fruit in your life. That is my promise" (4/2/86).

"You are all worthy to come to a loving God. No matter how terrible your sins may be, I can forgive them. And I am a God that forgets after I have forgiven. By accepting my cross, you have accepted discipleship in my name.

"You are worthy of salvation. So set aside your stubbornness and hardness of heart. Open your hearts to let in the light of my Spirit. Let me come in and show you your stubbornness. I want to give you fullness of life, fullness of freedom and deep and abiding joy. Open your hearts. Let the light of my Spirit come in. I walk with you; I heal you; I touch you with my love. Tell me the desires of your heart" (4/9/86).

"There are false prophets among you. I call you to listen with a discerning spirit to those who speak for some are not speaking my word. Do not be misled; my sheep should know their shepherd's voice. If you do not spend time with me daily and read my word daily, how will you recognize my voice? I tell you do not eat all the food handed to you. Test it first with me for I will never mislead you. You can trust me for I am a faithful God" (4/16/86).

CHAPTER 33

2008

"Can you hear me now? It is time, yet so few hear my voice. I call out, but who hears me? Why do you cry out when I have already gifted you? You are whole; you are my people; you have everything you need. Yes, you have boldness, fortitude, and strength. Release it and bring my people to me. My arms are open waiting to embrace my people. Lead them to me. Step out in faith. You have already received it. Go. Time is short" (8/16/08).

"You dance with such joy and praise; let me join you and give praise to the Father who loves you so. There, I am one with you. Lift your arms and feet in praise to the eternal Father. See what love the Father has for you that I will join you as his children, my brothers and sisters. You are mine and I am yours forever. Now sing and dance before my glory. I stand before you, your Lord, your God, and your brother" (9/7/08).

"You make a joyful voice to the Lord. Your praises pass through the three heavens to surround my throne with joy. You are my flock and

I send my angels to minister to you. What are your desires? What are your wants? Your praises touch my heart and I send my peace to you. Can you behold it? Let it become part of you. Let it be a sign to all that you are my people and I am with you forever" (9/14/08).

"How is your economy? Are you worried? Perhaps you listen to your media. You need to heed my media, my words. Have I not said to not be concerned about food or drink, your clothes or your job? Remember, I will never forsake you or abandon you.

Your storehouse is so finite; my storehouse is never empty. It awaits your call. Place your trust in me always for nothing is too big or too small. Consider what I can do with a few fish or a stormy sea. I can feed you and calm your fears, but you must trust me as your Lord. You don't have to look far for I live and dwell within you. Seek a quiet time and know my presence and seek what you need. I will hear your voice" (9/21/08).

"You are right to call me king, but my kingdom is not whole. It is fractured here and there, a piece here, a piece there. How I long for one kingdom, my bride. You are my people and I love you. Help me to further my kingdom in your midst. Do not think anything is too small or too spiritual. A cup of water and a healing are the same when it is done in love. And my love is so available to you to further and multiply it. Ask me and stretch forth your arm to proclaim my love. Pray, touch, move out; I am with you Fear not. Time is short" (9/28/08).

"What have you seen today? It is your world, but my world is not of this world. Let me show each of you my world where there is peace, love, and harmony. Wouldn't you long for that each and every day in your world?

"This is my view of the coming kingdom which was my thought from the beginning. You can help build my kingdom to tie together all the loose ends through my Son. Do not delay; do not hesitate. That impulse or nudge is my Holy Spirit, My brick builder. Can you see it? Can you see my kingdom coming together?

"I have given you so much for your city. Start there and let it gather steam and rapidly increase in structure and strength. Don't fear; I am leading you and you have only to hear my word and act on it, and it will be done" (9/30/08).

"Can you see my smile? Then you will know my happiness; how your praise and worship pleases me. Feel my love poured for you and on you for we are one, I in you and you in me. My glory is yours to know and nurture. There, I have decreed it. We are so close there is nothing to fear now or ever more. What shall overtake you when your praise binds us together? Don't lose sight of me and my love for you. It is enough for any worldly problems" (10/08/08).

"Oh what a time we will have together as you praise me and I gather you together to present you to the Father. You cannot know how much glory pervades the heavens. I love you, my flock, and your praise fills the heavens" (10/19/08).

"You ask for a sign. How can I give more than I have? I have given you that part of me which is my Son. He dwells in each of you. I have shown part of myself with each of you and have called you to be part of me. Rejoice; I live within you, not above or near you, but as part of you" (10/21/08).

"I am your rock in this time. I am not small enough to be ignored nor to be thrown away. I am large enough for you to walk around and wonder. But I want you to be part of me. I AM your rock. I will not be moved. My word is your promise, the rock of your Salvation.

"You can slip and fall from my rock unless you are firm in my word. I will not abandon you in this time. I will hold you tight. See I stand here and hold out my arms. Grab hold of me and trust me as your rock" (10/26/08).

"You are right that I am the lamb who was slain, but slain for you that we may be one. My glory I share with you and I dwell within you. Holy are you as I am holy.

"You please me with your praise. I truly inhabit the praises of my people as you, my people, are one with me. Never fear; never fret; never wonder. I am Lord—your Lord now and into eternity. Let loose and let me be even more of your lives. Let us be closer.

Have you not read that I dwell in you and you dwell in me? How much closer can we be? Don't limit me and you will see how much I want to be part of your lives" (11/2/08).

"You are right to call me holy, but I also see my holiness in you, my people. Yes, we are one and live in each other. How can this be? Look to me and observe my love.

"Are you fearful? I have conquered fear. Are you desperate? I am the source of your hope in all things. I am your Lord. Now in these times as always, I will be here for you. Inhabit my praises and let your smile and joy be a reflection of who lives and dwells in you" (11/16/08).

"As you lift your voices to praise me, I lift my voice to praise you to your Father and mine. Your praises reach the highest level of heaven and are so sweet to all who hear. Come before me always knowing I receive your love and praises. Never doubt me; never refuse my love for you as it is everlasting.

"If you don't believe you can see it, look at my people and know how I inhabit them as well as you. Worship me with an everlasting love I gave you. Let nothing interfere with our relationship in this day of troubles which I have conquered. Bring your concerns to me and let me present your troubles to your Father who loves you" (11/23/08).

"I call you beloved; I call you blessed, but I also call you my bride. Be ready. Time is short before the wedding. Soon all will be made clear. My light will penetrate the darkness and lead you to a feast in the clouds with your bridegroom.

"I say be ready. Do not be saddled with fears or doubts. I am in control of everything you see regardless of what you think or people tell you. I am your Lord and prophet and I tell you time is short. Believe it and be ready for a wedding as I have been planning it for eons" (12/08/08).

"Some of you come to honor a babe in the manger, but come to the manger; it is empty. Run to My tomb; it also is empty. I've grown up as your savior and Lord. You will not find me here or there, but only in my people as my kingdom is within my people.

"I have already given you my life as a gift that you might live. Now I give you my Spirit in fullness. If you have already received my glorious Spirit, be enriched; be refreshed; if not, let this Christmas be your Pentecost. I so desire you my people to be one with me. I want you to stretch forth your hands in peace, in healing, and in joy.

"Look around you—so many sad people. You are empowered to bring the joyous Christmas that so many desire. Tell them not to fear; I have already accomplished all they hope for. The baby grew up and became Lord, all powerful and all loving.

"Let this Christmas be so special as you let my love engulf you; let my love surround you; let my love permeate you; let my love be such a part of you that it will radiate to all about you. Let my love through you be the Christmas joy for all you meet. Let my gift of myself be your gift to all you meet" (12/21/08).

"A man in a red suit with reindeers brought peace and calm for a few minutes. Now we are back to normal life, but as Lord, my peace is a gift each day, each minute. My first gift was life for you; my second gift to you was my passion so I could live within you and you within me as in eternal life. My third gift is the baptism of my Holy Spirit. All my gifts are available" (12/28/08).

Chapter 34

2009

"You have grown in holiness and love of others. And your praise reaches me so forcefully and gentle, yet with zeal. I am so pleased with you. Now hear me; I want so much more from you but I will grant you so much more. You will go forth with new gifts, with stronger gifts for all people.

"Some of you worry how to touch others yet it is my Spirit who not only leads you but prepares them. You have only to obey. Yes, the harvest is ready. Look upon my gifts as your tools and bring me the harvest.

"Can you see me standing at the edge of the field? Look at me. I don't have scorn or a scowl on my face. No, you are my people, the laborers in my field. I await the fruits of your labors as you add to the kingdom.

"Now I will tell you something else: extend your hand; it is my hand. Look upon the poor with my eyes. Bless them; heal them; love them as I am part of you.

"When you come together as a community of prayer, I want you to know my presence. Perhaps you have not felt it before. From now on, you will know that I am your God and I am with you, my people. I expect you to know that I am present wherever you are and especially when you are all together" (1/7/09).

"You are right to sing I am holy, but know my holiness is reflected in you as you grow closer to me. This is the new life, growing closer to me, living in me and me in you. Do you know you are holy? Reflect on this as I dwell in you and you go forth to represent me. This is something you must realize that my gifts are available to you for my people. Extend yourselves; I will be with you. No action is too small or too big when we are involved together in ministry. Reflect on my love and let it overwhelm you as you consider how much all people need the love that you know. Don't hold back; extend my love to friends, family, and people you meet" (1/11/09).

"Are you totally free? That is my desire. That is why I died for you, not half-heartedly, but completely. My passion paid the price. I surrendered everything for you. I ask you to surrender to me to be born free of all entanglements" (1/18/09).

"Gather around while I tell you who I am. I am your friend as well as your Lord and I love you with an everlasting love. Yes, my love is everlasting as you are now living born again in eternity.

"I have told you I have more gifts for you. Be open and let my Spirit touch you. Once touched, share your gifts to transform my people. Do not hold back. Be bold and know I have laid the ground work. Your job is to plant; my job is to harvest and it is time" (1/22/09).

"I want your country to know my love flowing as sweet honey. Your laws were founded on my word. Now there are no standards as you have put my word aside, my eternal word for other beliefs, personal opinions and every ancient sin ever committed.

"Your many opinions will not solve your problems. You need my wisdom to even continue. Come humbly to me and I will respond. If you continue as present, you will know my wrath, bitterness as lemon rather than honey.

"I ask you to choose life; seek my favor and be blessed. Seek your wisdom and be cursed. I have spoken. If you doubt me, consult my word that you have discarded so easily. I love the contrite heart of a nation, but resist the pride and sinfulness of a Babylon" (1/25/09).

"Last week I was firm with you; not only you, but all Christians, for you need to get more active. It is harvest time and my holiness should be manifest throughout the land. Is it bottled up in you? Sow, sow, sow everywhere to everyone. Time is short and my kingdom door is open, not closed or revolving. Go forth and let my love guide you. I will not desert you for I am part of you and my Spirit urges you forth.

"This is not a time for timidity but boldness throughout the land from the inner city to the homeless, to the wealthy, to the countryside, to Christians and non-Christians alike. All are my people and need to know my love. Forget about your talents and rely on my gifts. Go forth; take my hand and let me guide you with my Spirit. Yes it is time" (2/11/09).

"Are you aware of what I am doing? Search my scriptures as I don't want you to be surprised about what is to come. Without knowledge of my plans, fear can try to gain a hold within you. But my love conquers any fear" (2/15/09).

"You talk about my presence and you have it for I live and dwell in each of you. I want you also to concentrate on my presents. Yes, it sounds the same, but you can have both as I have both.

"My indwelling and my gifts are what make you different from all other mankind who don't know me. Open up and allow me to be even more of your life. You cannot imagine the depth of my love as you open more and more. It is a matter of trusting me for I will honor your request" (3/3/09).

"My people I love you. You have brought honor and glory to me this weekend. Remember that as I have walked with your Arizona forefathers, I stand ready to walk with you. Time is short. The harvest they dreamed about is for your generation. You will not fail for how can you as I am with you. Therefore, fear not as I have conquered fear.

"You rightly call me Lord and God and sing my praises. I inhabit your praises as I in turn inhabit you, my people. Nothing is too small; nothing is too big for we are one. Ask what you will. Let me bless you with more desire, more fervor, more peace. Nothing is hidden from me nor not revealed to you. Step forth in boldness with my peace as I direct you.

"Don't look for opportunities. I will show you where to go and what to do. You are my light for a generation operating in the dark and blindness to my word. Go now: live, love and be ME to this generation" (3/1/09).

"Change? It won't come from me for my word is unchangeable. But if you aren't seeing me with spiritual eyes, you need spiritual glasses that my word may be part of you. Look about you, the things of this world bring much allure, but are so transitional. My world, both seen and unseen is forever. Come be part of me and my world for the time is now, not later when change might not be possible.

"Take your spiritual glasses and see my world created for you for all eternity. The present allure with conflicts and moral indecision will all fade away as my glory becomes more apparent. Come join me" (3/09/09).

"Is it time for my harvest in your life? Look around you. Among the many things you see, confusion is everywhere. Sometimes change is not right. I have given you the answer; it is my Son. Draw people close to you and tell them of my love, of salvation, of healing and the harvest beginning. Show them my love and tell them of his life. How there was no confusion in my Son's life. How he is a beam of hope and remains so forever.

"There is also no confusion in the kingdom. It is the refuge this kingdom needs but doesn't know. Tell them everywhere of my love and my direction. Tell them how my Son brings peace as confusion is put to rest forever. My people it is time for my harvest" (3/15/09).

"You praise me for my holiness. Do you know you are being transformed by my holiness for I live and dwell in you? This is your change as you become more and more like me. As your depth in holiness increases, so does your love for my people.

"I have called you to represent me in this area where you are building a storehouse of joy for all my people. Be open as I introduce new gifts into your lives. These are not changes from me but a deeper closeness between us. I long for you to know my presence and bring my gifts to others" (3/22/09).

"Do you see my goodness? It is difficult with the lust, greed, perversion and abominations pushed by the media. Look not only to me, but to each other for I long for you. I want my light to shine through you to attract so many people. If you ask more of whatever I have for you, I will answer you for you are my light in a world of darkness. Let my light shine through you. Be even a beacon so people will ask what you have: 'Why are you so happy with so much stress and such indecision everywhere?' Let your answer be that you know I AM and respond, 'Let me tell you about him'" (4/5/09).

"Thank you for honoring me this day of resurrection. I want this to be your resurrection also, free from guilt and doubt and filled with my love, power, and authority.

"This is a time of joy and my glory floods the earth. Do you perceive it or only have knowledge about all that I am? Let this be your resurrection. Come to me with all you have for my kingdom and let me transform you for even more of my glory. My desire is for you to be so complete that my resurrection power will draw others to you.

"Do you hear me? We are one; go forth with all I give you, all I am. I don't want you to practice my presence. I want you to know my presence as I live and dwell in you by my resurrection power" (4/12/09).

"Do you carry any guilt? Are you conscience of any guilt? Give it to me for I died so you would be free of guilt as all your sins are forgiven.

"Perhaps this was holding you back. You are now free so let go and let me be Lord. I promise you growth, love, and peace by my Spirit.

"We are one so how can there be anything negative in you? My glory I share with you as you are my light. If there is anything negative in you, it is not of me. Be confirmed in my will and reap the harvest I created for my people free of sin and enlightened by my Spirit" (5/3/09).

"This is a special day for me for I also was born of a mother who nurtured me, guided me and first taught me about love. Today I share my glory not only with mothers, but all my people. Let today be a day of joy for what I have accomplished for you means no fear and no stress for you. Your praises reaches me and I pour forth my love to you. Receive it and be nurtured and grow in my love.

"Are you one with me? If not, why not, for we are one family. I was born so we could be one and I invite you to let me increasingly become a greater part of your lives" (Mother's Day, 5/10/09).

"For two weeks now, you have praised me for my holiness according to my word. My holiness is there for you to have as my plan is to present you to the Father, holy and spotless. Can you receive my holiness? Of course you can. You have only to imitate my life and ask to receive my holiness. It is yours along with all my virtues and gifts for we are one, dwelling in each other. Can you not fathom the depth of my love for you to absorb and be transformed? Let this happen so your praise will shout, 'We are one, my God and I. He is Love and I am his Love, now and forever'" (5/31/09).

"It is a new day for my church, a day when my power is shown everywhere, where I will show my glory and where healing will be common and manifest. Are you with me as I pour forth my Spirit in a more powerful way to you who have chosen me? I tell you it will be glorious for you within my church. Things you have dreamed about will be commonplace. However, this is not a time to wonder if this is happening, but a time to step forth in my faith and make it happen for my glory. The time is now. Now is the time for what will come" (6/15/09).

"I am with you says the Lord. I am yours and you are mine. Be not afraid of what is coming soon. You and your families will be protected. Fear not. Keep your eyes on me. I am love and desire all men to love me, but my wish is not being fulfilled. Soon people will know my wrath for abandoning their God. Stay with me; be with me and yearn for me always" (6/25/09).

"You sing of my holiness and I marvel how you are becoming holy. Continue to draw deeper for my love and your growth will be continually increasing. Yes, I am holy and my desire is for you to be as holy as I am so I can present you to the Father. This is my joy—your perfection which is happening now. You might not be aware but through my Holy Spirit and my indwelling with you, it is a reality. Concentrate on my indwelling, my presence before you" (7/5/09).

"You sing of my glory and power. Do you realize I share these with you and I am your hope in everything? Come to me and let me use my power to cover your problem with my glory. What is too much for your God? Can you name anything I can't do or handle a problem for you? I created the world in a word. Is your problem so big? Therefore, let me be Lord; let my power and glory reside in you. Then your problems become our problems and you can concentrate on helping others which is the way of living in my kingdom. Come to me; let me love you and fill you to overflowing so my love will be visible in you and available to all you meet. Always remember the words, 'I am Yours, Lord'. Take a minute and know my presence no matter what the circumstance or where you are" (7/13/09).

"What is holiness? It is when my Spirit joins us and makes us one. But it has to be contagious to all my people for so many are alone and empty. Only my holiness can heal their hurt.

"Do not be afraid or timid to broadcast my holiness and how it is available for all. You are never full for I always have more for you to share and more for your own infilling. I said last week that you are holy. Believe it. Let my words be part of you as I share my holiness with you and you proclaim it throughout the city and to the nations. Yes, I am holy and it is also my gift to you" (8/23/09).

The word I have for you is "**TIME**."

"**T** is for temerity or boldness, the opposite of fear: fear of the enemy; fear of the future; fear for your loved ones. Attention: they were my loved ones first and still are! Remember, perfect love casts out fear. You need to grow in this area. The shaking that has been prophesized is almost upon you and you have to conquer fear now to live in my realm then.

"**I** is for is it going to happen? Most assuredly! I assure you my will be done. Everything must change so I can have a spotless bride. What do I have now? So many churches are like a mistress as they adapt to the world's rules and abandon my divine and eternal word."

"**M** is for mine. You are my people, not the governments; not Satan; not even some harlot church. We are talking about my people, my holy people. Yes, I realize there is a spiritual war going on to undermine my people. The mouth that roars against my people will soon be silenced."

"**E** is for easy. What do you think of the coming tide; will it be easy or hard? For non-believers, it will be impossible. For my people who put their trust in me, it will be easy. The task is mine, not theirs as it has always been my Lordship, my kingdom, and my people. You have only to trust me as Lord regardless of what happens and know that I am in control. No spirit or human being is in command; no army, church or denomination, no political party will rock my boat as I steer it myself.

"I promise you that I will not abandon you, but I call you to not abandon me for perilous times are almost here. Remember, you are mine and I hold you in the palm of my hand to protect you. But you must allow me to hold you if I am to be your Lord. Time is short as you will see. Your foes are everywhere and while you may not be able to see them, I do. Trust me to be Lord as that is my Father's command to me" (8/23/09).

"I rejoice in your praises so much that I want you to feel my presence within you as you honor me. My Holy Spirit is within you to confirm my love for you. Continue to praise and honor me as I am with you always. You have nothing to fear. Any concern should not be part of you. Your only concern should be the depth of my love. Is it increasing in you? I want a quantum leap of faith in me and will guide you. I am yours is not merely words. Right here and now feel my love within you to increase. That is something you will realize from now on" (8/9/09).

"Yes, I am a God of mercy. I tell you to call for my mercy on you for what is nearing is beyond your thoughts. However, you are my people and I will protect you.

"Call upon me for all your needs as I have always said. The time coming is a special time before my coming. I do not say it will be easy, but we will be together before we will be one forever.

"As I have said so many times, 'Fear Not,' regardless of happenings. I hold you and you are mine. Keep your eyes on me, not the world deteriorating around you. Remember, I am in charge" (9/6/09).

"You call me holy in your praises. Are you not holy due to the in filling of my Holy Spirit? It is time you realize who you are and the fullness of my love in you. If there is any doubt, come to me and let me show you my love. I will tell you of my life for you as it is related in scriptures. I want you to realize your power in me for it will be necessary to build my kingdom. Time is accelerating to my glory. Get ready. You are holy" (9/16/09*).*

"What does it profit a man if he gains the whole world? Look about you and see these people everywhere. It is greed, but greed isn't confined to absolute dollars and power. Greed can be a striving for something small, something electronic, maybe the latest gadget.

"There is nothing wrong with things. It is the mindset for acquisition that can be wrong. GOTTA HAVE is not my principle.

163

My plan is to seek our Father's will and be contented with his provisions. For some it will be riches to help spread the gospel; for others it will be a kitchen knife, but it will be our Father who supplies it.

"America is having a terrible time now with power, a faculty that should be mine and is my prerogative. Look about you and reflect on recent happenings. Are you happy with the money pool being evaporated on useless endeavors? Are you happy with the people who represent you?

"Is there cause to please me or to please demi-gods? You know I am not even part of the process. What I started, your country, has been abandoned. I tell you I am about to abandon your country, to lift the hand of my Spirit. When this happens, you will see the actions of a godless society multiplied beyond your imagination. Things will happen that mirror previous dictatorships.

"I will let you stay here for a while to witness how man can deteriorate without God; then I will take you home. The vision of me will be enough for you, but I will let you glimpse the absolute collapse of mankind without the restraining hand of my Spirit. Is it too late for change? Yes; pray that the time is short, but know your redemption is at hand" (9/20/09).

"You have endured months of blazing heat, but now my Spirit refreshes you in the natural and spiritual world. Get ready for I am about to pour forth my Spirit in new ways assisted by my angels to equip you as never before.

"You have prayed; you have waited; you have sought my counsel. I have heard your prayers and now proclaim a new era where we are one, you my people and I as we enflame the kingdom for my glory.

You will have everything you need, but you must have the desire. I will provide the rest and tell you my power will be demonstrated through you.

"I want my church transformed to reflect my glory so that all will know that I am Lord. Go forth; transform your church; transform your city; transform your land. I am with you to inspire you and equip you" (10/11/09).

"Today you have worshipped and praised me with a new intensity that is sweet to my ears. I encourage you to come to me each and every day in worship and praise. In this manner you will be free of so many trials and able to resist others. Come to me; you cannot imagine how much love I have for you and want to release it to each of you, yes, every one of you. Let me fill you as I am filled" (10/18/09).

"What is the breadth of my love? Can you measure my love as I measure yours? I tell you my love is without bounds and is infinite. It never rises nor falls. It is always there for you. As our Father loves me, so I love you and with the power of my Spirit, I have declared it. Tap into my love and let me imbue you with myself in deeper ways than you have experienced until now. Come, be one with me" (10/25/09).

"My glory is not hard to see. Look about you in your beautiful land that I created for you. Like everything I created reflects my glory, so in your quest for me, you reflect my glory.

"I gladly take you to our Father and present you as my gift to him. Can you not sense we are one? He and I, and you and I, all by the power of my Spirit. Bathe yourself in my glory so that you might reflect all that I am to all peoples. Do not be fearful and do not delay for I long to expand my church" (11/1/09).

COMMENTARY:

Holy Spirit, help us to sense we are one with you! Help us all to come into the realities of our oneness together. You have made it possible for us to know you by experiencing your glorious love! We drink of your love! We drink of your goodness and acceptance!! We drink of your light and life that sets us totally and completely free! Let all else melt away and let the pure reality of you overtake us now! It is for the praise of your glory, one in the knowledge of you in me and me in you! Fill the earth with it just as you promised you would do.

"Now look at what you are about to do. Are these my plans? I want to change your approach today as so many people are hurting. It is not only financial; it is spiritual and fear is such a part of Sunday's service. Know this and cast these negative spirits from my church. Then you can proceed with elevated worship once my people are free.

"Don't hesitate to loosen these binds that hold back my people. They are good folks but are held in bondage they don't know about. As you come forth, examine their faces; see their moods. Free them and let my glory come forth. I want them to know me; feel my presence, and see my glory. But this can only happen as they are first renewed. And don't you be fearful either. I now give you the insight and power to free my people. I desire freedom for my people, then worship will reach new heights" (11/15/09).

"You are *my* Thanksgiving for I give thanks for your praises, your worship, and how you seek me. I can tell you I can always be found in your hearts and in your praises.

"Do not fear anything. I am your God and I love my people and take care of them, you as well as others. Now I ask you for something. Get to know each other in a deeper way for you will need each other even more in the coming times. I will be with you, but I want you to be close to each other for support. This isn't a matter of end times as much as being my brothers and sisters for I want you to be closer. In this manner you will share the various joys and graces I give each of you.

"These are tokens of my love and are meant to be shared in order to appreciate how much I love each of you, my wonderful people" (11/29/09).

"Much of the world awaits my birth while I await the world to be reborn. Look around you and perceive the elements that bring sadness to my heart. I did what my Father asked so the people could live. Yes, they were alive for centuries, yet pursue other kingdoms today. Now I depend on you to spread my light.

"I call you to a growth you cannot imagine. Do not be satisfied with the present happiness and power you perceive. My gift to you has always been my Spirit, not wrapped up, not restrained, but unlimited for you to build my kingdom in your church, in your city, wherever you are. You are my bright lights this Christmas. Shine forth with my love to all you meet. Extend your hand of peace and know it is my hand to heal my people. You are not alone. I was born and my life given that you would enjoy our companionship within you for you to build my church in power and love. Do not look for the manger. Look at my empty cross and know the power I have given you" (12/6/09).

"Why are you waiting? I have given you everything you need. I wait for you to breakout in worship, praise, prophecy, and healings as you have never known. This is my vision for you. How much longer must I wait for you to hear and believe my word?

"I am all for you; be all for me and let my church explode with my love and blessings. I don't want it to be a secret anymore. Let it come. Take a step and I will magnify the blessings" (12/20/09).

CHAPTER 35

2010—BUILDING THE KINGDOM

"What is the New Year? It is not just another one of opportunities, but the year of increased power. You will dream dreams, have visions, know my presence and realize my power in you. As you daily draw closer to me, you will become more aware of our friendship and how much I want to accomplish through you.

"At times you may feel alone, but this is a false feeling and only a feeling. Have I not told you I live and dwell in you? This is not ON/OFF, but always. Be aware and do not doubt my love and my presence. Stretch forth your hand in love and healing power and know it is I motivating you.

"Develop your hearing so you will know my voice. My spirit speaks softly to you. Learn to hear him and follow his advice, his yearning, and his plan for you. Never doubt you are my Father's son, my brother, and my Spirit's friend. Not that many people know this. Therefore, love my people as I do and bring them to me" (1/10).

"You honor me with your praise, but I want so much more. I want your heart to know my love. I want your thoughts so we can be friends. I want your hands to extend my love. Do you not see how

169

a father longs for his children and wishes them well? I tell you that you have hardly begun to tap into all I have for you.

"You are playing with my gifts as toys and I have gold for you. You can't build the kingdom by playing with toys now and then with others. I see you as bricks building my kingdom. Do you? My edifice has already started but I need it finished. It is time for the harvest into my kingdom and time flies more than you know.

"Come to me and I will equip you with my power for you are only toying with it now. You please me, but I want you so much more powerful for my name's sake.

"What does Jesus mean daily? To some, it is only a word; to others it is an exclamation. To you, my Son is power, life, the truth, and the way. Explain this to people who are neutral in their faith. This is not a simple desire of mine but a command to build the kingdom" (1/17/10).

"I want you to view my people a new way. Do not be concerned with externals as how they look; how they are dressed or where they live, nor what race they are. Forget all the material things that might influence you. Look upon my people as I do. It is only their soul and spirit that matter. I created everyone and look upon everyone with love. Do I love someone from Scandinavian any more than someone from Africa? Obviously not. Therefore, look upon all with my eyes as someone who needs love. The super-rich need my love just as the super poor. Without me, what is their life but a collection of things or a quest for necessities? You are my smile; you are my touch; you are my healing hand. I have given you all you need by my Spirit. Now take my eyes and see as I see. You will not see someone beautiful nor someone bedraggled, but someone who needs a ticket to my kingdom. My Son is the ticket and he lives within you. Go forth like the disciples of old and build my kingdom. Jesus is the example and he said you will do mightier things. The harvest awaits you for you have the light to share. Go forth" (1/24/10).

"We approach the second month of the year. What has happened to prepare my kingdom? Are you wiser? Are you happier? Are you prepared for the forthcoming battle?

"Prepare my people for growth in my Spirit. Some talk of my power and presence. I want all to experience my gifts. There must be a change so that my Spirit is like a rushing wave over the people. You talk about change, but it is like a drip so far. I want a torrential downpour on all my people.

"Let My gifts flow in abundance to all who come. Be open. My Spirit is ready like a rushing wind to touch everyone. Pray, praise, and be open, open to my desires for your growth" (1/10).

"You may think this only a day for spouses and their children or those deeply in love. This is a special day as I send my Holy Spirit so you can love with the depth of my love. I want you to know the depth of my love for all each day and not just on one special day. "Extend my love; extend my peace and tell of salvation. Look upon me as a mother hen gathering all her little ones. I desire this so I can cover everyone with my shed blood to cleanse them. The heart is a symbol today and I gave my heart for all mankind to be free from earthly woes, to know my eternal love. Stretch forth your hand everyday with my love so all will be my people" (Valentine's Day, 2/14/10).

"Woe to those who don't know me and hide from me. I desire all mankind for my bride. Can you imagine the sorrow for what I created and they don't know me nor do they want me? Even with you, my people, I do not want your toe dipped in the water. This is like a trial rather than a commitment. I want all of you. My desire is for a baptism of water and a baptism of the fire of my Spirit. Only then are you my warriors, part of my army to cleanse this generation.

"Be politically correct for me. My name is Jesus and I am Lord. 'I am the Way, the Truth, and the Life.' Time gets shorter and shorter and my people are missing my salvation in favor of the temporary earthly allures. Do not be mesmerized by false lights. As I was the light of the world when among you, you are now my lights. Let my Spirit shine forth in you and let yourself be the mirror of my love and goodness. I have called you. You are mine and I will not fail you" (3/7/10).

"Today I see a new you. Do you sense it as I do? I have poured forth my Spirit. Maybe you don't feel a new presence, but I tell you that you will increase in fervor, holiness, and spirituality. Your eyes will be redirected to build my kingdom" (3/14/10).

"Today you rise with me to new heights. Take my hand as I reveal new delights. This is a time of joy, my joy for you as you accept my passion and resurrection and are restored to the kingdom. I have completed our Father's wishes and now it is your turn to accept your inheritance purchased with my blood.

"Behold I make all things new and today is that day for this community. You will have a new feeling of joy as my Spirit envelopes you now and evermore. It is time to enlarge my kingdom and you are part of the building. Be not timid but forthright in your outlook. I have given you the tools. Be my warriors as well as my builders" (4/4/10).

"There is much joy here today and your praise reaches to the heavens. You are growing steadily in my love, but I have so much more to give, so much more to teach you. Keep your eyes on me for the world's distractions will increase daily. Therefore, my cure and aid is the daily reading of my word.

"I AM the Word, but you need the daily infusion of my word, the scriptures, so that my Spirit can guide you through this maze that has been formulated as diversity and so many other false names.

"Keep your eye on me and let me continue to guide you. I know where you are going and I'm guiding you there step by step.

"I delight in your growth; let my joy permeate your being. In this manner, you will be the lights that I call you to be. You please me in your daily growth so don't despair nor grow weary. Stand firm as a light I have created in the midst of the world's darkness around you" (2010).

"I am your shepherd and you are my flock. You are my brothers and sisters led by me, not rounded-up by others. You are a living part of my body. You are a flock of warriors, Spirit-Filled warriors building my kingdom. Is this how you see yourself? If not, it is not my word or desire. If you are troubled, you are not listening to my Spirit for I freed your soul from sin and false spirits.

"My desire is that you are my light for a world gone godless. Be my flock known for godliness. In this manner bring my love and healing power to a restless generation, a people grown cold without love. I am the solution to any problem and I long to help. I can help you or I can help others through your prayers.

"Watch out for marauding wolves masquerading with other voices. Remember, I have made you warriors to build my kingdom. You are not powerless, gentle sheep. Let these words be fixed in you that you may know I am with you and want you to go forth boldly, powerfully, and yet extending my love" (2/10).

"I am your Lord and God. Forever praise me and let me share my glory with you. Do not be afraid to let go and let me surprise you with love you cannot imagine. I am not limited by time, space, or material. All I have is inexhaustible. What do you need? Humbly ask me and I will reply. I am your mighty God. Trust me and become one with me for I long for you so much. Do not drag or delay the fullness of my love. I have promised it and I long for you to receive my fullness" (3/10).

"Because I am your Lord and God, I will tell you something: My love does not have an ebb and flow: it is not up and down; it is not here and there. I AM Love. Regardless of your actions, my love is always there. I want you to know the simple truth that you are always loved by me. Have I not died for you and sent my Spirit? Have I not said I will dwell in you? Like you, I am the Father's Son. You are children of God because you chose me.

"Remember this: you have an eternal love within you. I call you to radiate that love to a world where love is fleeting and conditional. My love in you is a perfect love. Therefore, touch all my people with me. As you touch my peoples, I am with you to guide you and help you. You don't have to be afraid to reach out because it is I who guides you. I want my kingdom to grow and I chose my body as the tools for the building. I will supply the mortar and you the bricks. Start building" (7/11/10).

"You grope for ways to reach me. You use old clichés, but fail in every attempt. Do you not know I am among you? I hear you, but I want a change of heart; I desire openness to all, not a weekly monologue. Why aren't the truths shared with the body, my body by the way?

"Some ask, where are the miracles? I say they are in my hand ready to be distributed, but first there have to be some turnarounds. Let my people go was not for a time before. It is also my way of saying what is wrong in my churches. If you don't recognize it, I call it absolute leadership that belongs only to me. Unless there is a change, the buildings will fall and the people drift away.

"The church will begin to crumble bit by bit by my direction. Most people will not notice until it is too late. The glory and pomp will gradually decrease until it is just a shell. I will offer the people my Spirit. Some will accept him, but most will reject him, preferring to stay with rituals and rules which do not bring them to me. Now to my faithful, I will also promise my Holy Spirit, but in a new way, a way of power, of visible power and healing to bring people to my kingdom.

"I say time is short; work therefore to bring the strays into my kingdom. Have no fear for I am not only with you, but in you. Stretch forth your hand; it is me guiding you. Pray to our Father; it is me guiding you.

"You have worked for my kingdom before. The difference now is that I am guiding you with power. Go forth to see, to heal, to conquer the evil one. Let it be known that I am Lord" (10/10/10).

COMMENTARY:

I believe God has instructed me to share what he has spoken in this word. Pray that God will cleanse all denominations by his Spirit.

"You sing about opening the floodgates of heaven. Do you not perceive the time? I am poured forth; my glory is upon my people to attract others to my kingdom. Time is short, but my favor is upon you. Do not question; go forth with my power. So many need my love, but don't know it and are in circles with the allure of the world. Tell them of my love" (12/19/10).

CHAPTER 36

2011-2012 YEARS OF DECISION

"I see a spark; I want a fire; I see droplets; I want a torrent of my love. I am ready. Tap into my love and achieve the growth I desire. I need warriors in this time. Are you ready? Come to me expecting me to do what I desire. But I need your faithful attention and strong desire. I will act if you come to me. Become warriors for my kingdom. Let my Spirit be a torrential flood for your spirit. I want to enflame you" (1/23/2011).

"I have seen your world and it is wanting. Do you doubt this? Look around you regardless of what the media tells you.

"Read my word and learn what I have already told you. Now, where do we go from here? You need to put your absolute trust in me for different times are coming as I have said before. But stay with me as I am with you always regardless of problems in your world" (1/30/2011).

"When my people gather together for a meal, am I not there with you? I will be there to enjoy your joy of being together for this is my

Spirit working in each of you. For today, my word is to be watchful this year for this is one of decision in view of problems. You will be tested, not by me, but by the economy, by the food chain, by lawlessness, and the gain in immorality as though it is moral. Fear not; I am with you to guide you, to sustain you, and enrich you. Let me be the sweetness in your life so the world can see me in you. Do not doubt my love or my concern for you and remember my storehouse has many treasures for you and it is never locked. Ask and you will receive" (2011).

"Be biblical detectives searching out my meanings. You need to be grounded in my word. When attacked, I didn't argue with the evil one; I used scripture. The same pertains to you for you will be tested, not by me, but by other forces, both human and spiritual. I will always be with you and my Spirit will equip you" (2011).

COMMENTARY:

When Jesus was attacked by the evil one, He didn't quote the New Testament as it had not been written yet. He quoted from the Old Testament.

"Do not take the easy attitude that things will stay the same. Look about you; things are not the same. Everything is changing and not for the good. My church must be the light in the cesspool of darkness called the modern age. Be the light and bring my light to people. My kingdom is within you. I call you to be travel agents to enlist people in my kingdom before the journey takes place. Regardless of circumstances about to happen, I am with you and will protect you" (2011).

"Pay attention to the world's decline in every area. Everything is changing and will continue due to frequency and intensity. Come closer to me for knowledge and protection. To survive, you must trust me. I call you my people, but you must act like my people and know my ways.

"This is a great time for the deceiver so stay grounded in my word. My Spirit will guide you, so stay open. The coming tide will overflow the world, but my kingdom will be glorious in my name. Stay with me and survive" (3/11).

"Be on guard for the enemy is increasing his foul tactics everywhere. He desires to thwart my revival and renewal of my people. You must warn them not to be deceived. The world is crashing, but I will not be overcome nor will my people if they follow my word. Stay focused on me and my plans. Forget the media who are so variable from day to day. Do not heed the allure of the world. Keep your eyes focused on me.

"The next year and a half will draw you to the TV like a magnet for the political battles. Stay grounded in my word and my desires and do not let the electronic negativity, immorality, and greed be part of your lives.

"I am the Savior and am totally correct for my Father and not politically correct for any happening. I assure you tough times are coming, but will not affect you if you work with me and stay connected to my word. He who has eyes to see should keep His eyes on me and not the verbal conflicts happening everywhere" (4/24/2011).

"Today I have risen and you have also risen with me. Will you leave the worldly strings that hold you back from being completely one with me? I desire not only you, but I desire so much from you. You are my people and you need to be my light to a world growing darker by the day. Some people have spoken of things being shaken. That is too mild for they should have said things are crashing. How can things be rebuilt unless they crash?

"Look around you and see that everything material or immaterial must be redone in my world. I will refresh my world, but terrible things will happen first. Yes, the world has progressed so much it must crash for the light to be revealed in its midst. And you are the light I have chosen. Let your light shine forth with brightness and not just a glimmer now and then. People need a beacon to guide them and to run to. My church is supposed to be that refuge of love and truth. Welcome these folks with open arms and know my love will pour forth from you by my Spirit" (Easter-2011).

"Today I want you to know me in a new way as friend and companion. I am not miles away. I am with you and always beside you to guide you. Talk to me as your close friend. Share your joy as well as your sorrows with me" (4/29/2012).

"My people, I recognize your holiness and call you to growth; yes, become even closer to me. I desire all of you to build my kingdom. Do not say, 'I am not qualified'; you have my Holy spirit for anything I command you. Do not say you don't have the experience; you have my wisdom. Do not say, 'I am too old or too young'; my Spirit is ageless and will equip you.

My kingdom awaits your ministry. Feel my presence now and know that I am with you as you go forth. You will never be alone with your Father smiling down on you, with me praying for you and my Spirit guiding you. Help build my kingdom'" (9/2/2012).

CHAPTER 37

THE DIRECTION OF
PROPHECY IN SCRIPTURE

It really isn't possible to summarize the bible in a few headings, but here are some key elements.

GOD'S CALL

- "Then I heard the voice of the Lord saying, 'Whom shall I send? Who will go for us?' "Here I am, I said; send me" (Isaiah 6:1-8).
- "Before I formed you in the womb, I knew you; before you were born, I dedicated you, a prophet to the nations I appointed you" (Jer. 1:4-10).
- "To him, all the prophets testify, saying that everyone who believes in him, he forgives of sins through his name" (Acts 10:43).

TIMELESS PROPHECIES (FOR THE FIRST CENTURY A.D. AS WELL AS THE TWENTY-FIRST CENTURY)

- "Reform your lives! The Reign of God is at hand" (John the Baptist-Matt. 3:2b).

- "Reform your lives! The kingdom of heaven is at hand" (Jesus-Matt. 4:17).
- "Save yourself from this generation which has gone astray" (Acts: 2:40b).
- "For the time will come when people will not tolerate sound doctrine, but, following their own desires, will surround themselves with teachers who tickle their ears. They will stop listening to the truth and will wander off to fables" (2 Timothy 4:3-4).

GOD'S FAITHFUL LOVE

- "For thus says the Lord God:" I myself will look after and tend my sheep" (Ezekiel 34:11-16).
- "When Israel was a child, I loved him; out of Egypt I called my son" (Hosea 11:1-4).

THE PRAISE OF GOD

- "To whom can you liken me as an equal?" says the Holy One. "Lift up your eyes on high and see who has created these" (Isaiah 40:25-26).
- "O Lord, you are my God, I will extol you and praise your name, for you have fulfilled your wonderful plans of old" (Isaiah 25:1).

THE PROMISE OF SALVATION

- "I will put my Spirit in you that you may live, and I will settle you upon you land. Thus, you shall know that I am the Lord. I have promised, and I will do it says the Lord" (Ezekiel 37:1-14).

- "Then afterward I will pour out my Spirit upon all mankind" (Joel 3:1).
- "Yes, God so loved the world that he gave his only Son that whoever believes in him may not die but may have eternal life" (John 3:16).
- "There is no salvation in anyone else, for there is no other name in the whole world given to men by which we are to be saved" (Acts 4:12).

GOD'S JUSTICE

- "Trample my courts no more! Bring no more worthless offerings" (Isaiah 1:13a).
- "You have been told, oh man, what is good, and what the Lord requires of you: only to do the right and to love goodness, and to walk humbly with your God" (Micah 6:6-8).

GOD'S MERCY

- "All, from the least to the greatest shall know me says the Lord, for I will forgive their evildoing and remember their sins no more" (Hebrews 8:11-12).
- "Come now, let us set things right, says the Lord: Though your sins be like scarlet, they may become white as snow" (Isaiah 1:11-17).
- "All men are now undeservedly justified by the gift of God through the redemption wrought in Christ Jesus. Through his blood, God made him the means of expiation for all who believe" (Romans 3:24-25).

FALSE PROPHECY

- "Listen not to the words of your prophets who fill you with emptiness, visions of their own fancy. They speak not from the mouth of the Lord" (Jeremiah 23:16).
- "Be on your guard against false prophets, who come to you in sheep's clothing, but underneath are wolves on the prowl. You will know them by their deeds" (Matthew 3:15).

LAST DAYS

- "Do not forget this: there will be terrible times in the last days. Men will be lovers of self and of money, proud, arrogant, abusive, disobedient to their parents, ungrateful, profane, inhuman, implacable, slanderous, licentious, brutal, hating the good. They will be treacherous, reckless, pompous, lovers of pleasure rather than of God as they make a pretense of religion but deny its power. Stay clear of them" (2 Timothy 3:1-5).

CHAPTER 38

THE FUTURE

There are numerous works proving that Jesus is the Messiah and fulfilled the messianic prophecies in the Old Testament. In addition, as the Son Of God, Jesus is the supreme prophet. Therefore, his words have a special meaning in scripture. As we near the end of this book, I thought it would be interesting to consider what Jesus said about the future.

ATTITUDE

"I assure you, unless you change and become like little children, you will not enter the kingdom of God" (Matthew 18:2b).

GROWTH

"How much more will the heavenly Father give the Holy Spirit to those who ask him" (Luke 11:13b).

"You will receive power when the Holy Spirit comes down on you" (Acts 1:8).

"God is Spirit and those who worship him must worship in Spirit and truth" (John 4:24).

HEAVEN

"When people rise from the dead, they neither marry nor are given in marriage, but live like angels in heaven" (Matthew 22:30).

RAPTURE

"I solemnly assure you, an hour is coming, has indeed come, when the dead shall hear the voice of the Son of God and those that have heeded it shall live" (John 5:25).

SALVATION

"I tell you the truth; no one can see the kingdom of God unless he is born again" (John 3:3—NIV).

"The man who believes in it (i.e. the gospel) and accepts baptism will be saved; the man who refuses to believe in it will be condemned" (Mark 16:16).

"Herein is love, not that we loved God, but that he loved us and sent his Son to be the propitiation for our sins" (1 John 4:10).

SECOND COMING

"The Son of Man will come with his Father's glory accompanied by his angels. When he does, he will repay each man according to his conduct" (Matthew 16:27).

"If a man is ashamed of me and my doctrine, the Son of Man will be ashamed of him when he comes in glory and that of his Father and his holy angels" (Luke 9:26).

"The coming of the Son of Man will repeat what has happened in Noah's time. In the days before the flood, people were eating and drinking, marrying and being married, right up to the day Noah entered the ark. They were very unconcerned until the flood came and destroyed them. So will it be at the coming of the Son of Man" (Matthew 24:37-39).

"When you hear about wars and threats of wars, do not yield to panic. Such things are bound to happen, but this is not yet the end. Nation will rise against nation, one kingdom against another. There will be earthquakes in various places and there will be famine" (Mark 13:7-8).

SUSTENANCE

"Do not worry about your livelihood, what you are to eat or drink, or use for clothing" (Matthew 6:25a).

"Your heavenly Father knows all that you need. Seek first his kingship over you, his way of holiness, and all these things will be given you besides" (Matthew 6:32b-33).

WEARY

"Come to me, all you who are weary and find life burdensome and I will refresh you" (Matthew 11:28).

CHAPTER 39

PROPHETIC SUMMARIES

As the researcher, I have chosen a few of the modern prophecies that summarize various topics. I have not listed the date they were given above, as I believe they are timeless. I trust these words of the Holy Spirit will bless you and empower meditation.

ETERNITY

"What is forever? It is a moment with me that never ceases. You already know how to praise me, how to love me and accept my love. But forever began when you accepted me. It never stops yet seems like only a minute for we share such oneness. I long for you as you long for me, yet we are one in spite of such longing and desire. Now I will tell you something—there is so much more of my infinite love that you cannot imagine. You think you know love now; I tell you it has just begun for I have so many things planned for my people. You will be amazed at the depth of my love for those who up to now aren't even aware of my love. Help me build the kingdom to join you as friends and fellow believers. I will help you. Fear not."

GROWTH

"You are in my heart. Come follow me, I will show you the way. Do not walk too fast for you will only stumble. Do not be afraid for I will guide you in my wisdom. Take little steps and make them firm and secure so that they may re-enforce the next ones. I am leading you gently as only I can. You may think you are small, but you are an intricate and essential part of my eternal plan that only I know. Do not be led astray by others. Follow the leadings of my Spirit, for you know him. My plan for you is different than for all others. You are to grow and blossom as flowers, all different, but still flowers giving forth different fruit, but all for my glory. Do not say I wish I were a rose or a tulip, but know yourselves and grow in what I have given you. You together have a job in my great plan. Follow my lead and with all I give, you will know my will, for I love you and will share good things with you forever if only you follow me in love. Hear my words and rejoice for I am the Lord God of hosts and power."

DISCIPLESHIP

"I come to you tonight asking you to let my word into your life. Let me fight these battles that are yours. It saddens me when you try to fight them yourself. Turn to me and I will deliver you. I will deliver you like I delivered my people, Israel. Turn to me and I will guide you and set you free.

   "I love you; I want you to know that but I call you to be disciples and you do nothing. I call you to go forth as disciples and you do nothing. Time grows short and I want you to go forth in the power of my Spirit. I have many things I need to accomplish through you. I need you to do my will. I want you to hear me. Hear my voice and act on it. You are not to worry; you are only to listen to me. To hear me is to know my will. To know my will is to be one with me."

THE CHOICE

"I give you a command now that you must stop putting feet in both worlds. You must commit yourself now to one or the other. You must make your choice: You either commit yourself to me: to live that life to the fullest with no holding back or you commit yourself to the world. This is your choice. I allow you to have that choice freely, but I'm there as a loving Father. I'm there with arms wide open, but I want those hearts of yours and I want you to be sincere. Stop trying to thread the needle of two worlds. Make your choice."

HEALING

"My Spirit proclaims healing and my Spirit dwells in each of you and I call you tonight to proclaim this healing to others, to bring my healing to others. You are leaving my children in sickness. You are leaving them with broken spirits because you are not proclaiming this gift that I have given you, this power that is within you. It is my power; it is your power through me. Keep this in mind. Use what I have given you. My love gift is healing to my people. This is as great a gift to them as the love that I bear them. Do you understand?"

END TIMES

"Pay attention to the world's decline in every area. Everything is changing and will continue due to frequency and intensity. Come closer to me for knowledge and protection. To survive, you must trust me. I call you my people, but you must act like my people and know my ways.

"This is a great time for the deceiver so stay grounded in my word. My Spirit will guide you, so stay open. The coming tide will overflow the world, but my kingdom will be glorious in my name. Stay with me and survive."

BE PREPARED

"Be biblical detectives searching out my meanings. You need to be grounded in my Word. When attacked, I did not argue with the evil one; I used scripture. The same pertains to you for you will be tested, not by me, but by other forces, both human and spiritual. I will always be with you and my Spirit will equip you."

CHAPTER 40

QUO VADIS

We have examined various life styles resulting in up or down destinies. Therefore, it is time to ask, "Where *are* you going? Heaven and Hell are both realities for consideration.

Jesus stated that we can not serve two masters (i.e. secularism or spiritual living) at the same time (Matthew 6:24). Paul restated this as, "Do not conform yourself to this age, but be transformed by the renewal of your mind" (Romans 12:2a).

Paul also explained God's perspective. "He will repay every man for what he has done: eternal life to those who strive for glory, honor, and immortality by patiently doing right; wrath and fury to those who selfishly disobey the truth and obey wickedness. Yes, affliction and anguish will come upon everyman who has done evil . . . . But there will be honor, glory, and peace for everyone who has done good . . . ." (Romans 2:6-10). "Choose life" was the emphatic outcry in Deuteronomy 30:19b.

While there are consequences for our decisions, the overall theme of this book is about God's love for us and his quest for our eternal companionship. We have reviewed the spiritual gifts that God has made available and examined a personal relationship with Jesus. Furthermore, we presented 35 years of prophecies from a variety of sources. The purpose in presenting them was to show

God's love for his people. Overall, the hope is to grow in his love and to touch other people.

I trust that you have been able to meditate on some of these prophecies and realize God's love in a deeper way. We have talked about the Baptism of the Spirit as a method to release the gifts in your life. The prayer below seems to capture all the leanings toward a mature growth in the spiritual life.

Prayer for the Baptism of the Spirit by Fr. John Bartolucci (Used with permission)

Jesus I love you
I am sorry for my sins
I thank you for dying on the cross
for me personally
I celebrate your resurrection this beautiful day
by giving my life to you.
I invite you into my life,
Into my home, into my business,
Into my school, into my recreation,
into wherever I am.
Come, Lord Jesus
I truly accept you as my Lord
and my God and my personal Savior.
Come now and fill me with your Spirit,
fill me, Lord Jesus, with your Holy Spirit.
Fill me Lord Jesus with your love
and send me forth to my family and friends
to be able to share with them

your love and your concern.
Jesus, I love you
and I shall follow you
as your disciple every day of my life.

The Final Word

One of my friends, involved in charismatic renewal and pastoral activities for almost forty years, summarized all she heard in prophecies and what she saw Jesus continuously say as:

"I love you; I am with you; trust me."

PART 5

APPENDIX

CHAPTER 41

AFTERWORD

Recently, I saw a movie about a child prodigy. Reflecting about the movie, I wondered if this approbation would also apply to Christians regardless of our age. If we are God's children, could we become prodigies?

In God's kingdom, childhood is very important. It is a matter of attitude rather than age. It is childhood trust versus adult sophistication. Jesus said, "I assure you that whoever does not accept the reign of God like a little child shall not take part in it" (Mark 10:15).

The question then becomes how do we become children of God? Then how do we become prodigies? Paul explained this in one of his letters: "I will welcome you and be a Father to you and you will be my sons and daughters says the Lord God Almighty" (2 Cor. 6:18). Jesus explained the first criteria for the spiritual life to Nicodemus as being born again as this choice enables us to become prodigies in the spiritual world (John 3:3).

The apostle, John, writes that we *are* children of God (1 John 3:1-2). He also gives us the ultimate proof: "When anyone acknowledges that Jesus is the Son of God, God dwells in him and he in God" (1 John 4:15). With this new lifestyle, the Holy Spirit is an intimate part conferring knowledge. "I will tell you things great beyond reach of your knowledge" (Jeremiah 33:3). John also explains, "But you have the anointing that comes from the Holy One so that all knowledge is yours" (1 John 2:20). In case we missed the point, John restates, "The anointing you received from him remains in your hearts. This means that you have no need for anyone to teach you. Rather, as his anointing teaches about all things-and is true-free from any lie, remain in him as that anointing taught you" (1 John 2:27).

Are you following this? As God's children, we can be equipped to do what Jesus did on earth. Yes, we can become child prodigies, God's own prodigies, regardless of our age. Being born again and Spirit-filled, we have the opportunity to become prodigies.

In *Gifted* we have reviewed prophetic love and various gifts God makes available. God *is* glorified by us using his gifts to build his kingdom.

ADDITIONAL SCRIPTURAL REFERENCES

ITEM	BOOK/CHAPTER /VERSE
OLD TESTAMENT	
Spiritual Gifts	Isaiah 11:1-3
Sins to Avoid	Leviticus 18:6-23; 19:31; 20:6-21
NEW TESTAMENT	
Spiritual Gifts	Romans 12:6-8; Corinthians 12:6-10; Ephesians 4:11; 1 Peter 4:11
Fruit of the Spirit	Galatians 5:22
Sins to Avoid	Galatians 5: 20-21, 5:26; Corinthians 6:9-10 Romans 1:22-31; Colossians 3:5; 1 Peter 4:3
Another Gospel	Galatians 1:8

ABOUT THE AUTHOR

The author attended St. Mary's University where he received a major letter for journalism. He graduated from the Pontifical Institute of Philosophy with graduate studies at DePaul University and additional studies at Franciscan University. He worked for GTE as a staff engineer and with Texas Instruments as a research engineer and an account manager. He served in the United States Air Force Reserve for eight years.

He retired early to expand a writing career, which he still enjoys. He was Historic Editor of Excellence Magazine and wrote for numerous magazines as a Contributing Editor and raced sports cars for a few years. He was active in church work as a parish representative, parish council president, and co-pastor of a charismatic prayer group. He and his wife enjoy travel, photography and living in the Southwest.

WORKS BY THE AUTHOR

Ferrari Racing in the Midwest-2006—co-authored with David Seielstad. The work was serialized by chapter in Cavallino Magazine.

A Gilded Walk—The Path to Heaven: 2010

In addition, the author wrote hundreds of magazine articles that appeared in American, European, and Japanese magazines. He won four medals for journalism.

BIBLIOGRAPHY

Austin, Jill. *Dancing With Destiny.* Grand Rapids, MI: Chosen, 2007.

Beacham, Doug. *Plugged Into God's Power.* Lake Mary, FL: Charisma House, 2002.

Brandt/Corita. *Psalms Now.* St. Louis, MO: Concordia, 1973.

Brandt/Corita. *Epistles Now.* St. Louis, MO: Concordia, 1974.

Brandt/Corita. *Jesus Now.* St. Louis, MO: Concordia, 1978.

Brandt/Corita. *Prophets Now.* St. Louis, MO: Concordia, 1979.

Cerullo, Morris. *The New Anointing.* San Diego,CA: Morris Cerullo, 1975.

Clark, Steve. *Baptized in the Spirit and Spiritual Gifts.* Pecos, NM: Dove Publications, 1976.

Copeland, Kenneth. *John G. Lake.* Fort Worth, TX: Kenneth Copeland Publications, 1994

DeGrandis, Robert. *The Healing Ministry.* Texas: Praising God Catholic Association of Texas, 1985.

Harlow, Duane. *Breaking Out Of Religious Christianity*: Shippensburg, PA: Destiny Image Publishers, 2006

Hyatt, Eddie L. *2000 Years of Charismatic Christianity*: Lake Mary, FL: Charisma House, 2002.

Johnson, Bill. *When Heaven Invades Earth*: Shippensburg, PA: Treasure House, 2003

MacNutt, Francis. *The Nearly Perfect Crime*: Grand Rapids, MI: Chosen, 2005

McDermott, Gerald. *A Gilded Walk:* Bloomington, IN: iUniverse, 2010

Munroe, Myles. *Rediscovering The Kingdom*: Shippensburg, PA: Destiny Image, 2004

Pickett, Fuchsia. *Understanding the Personality of the Holy Spirit*: Lake Mary, FL: Charisma House, 2004

Pickett, Fuschia. *Walking in the Anointing of the Holy Spirit:* Lake Mary, FL: Chrisma House,

Pickett, Fuchsia. *Cultivating the Gifts of the Spirit*: Lake Mary, FL: Charisma House, 2004

Pickett, Fuchsia. *Presenting the Holy Spirit:* Lake Mary, FL: Creation House, 1997

Robertson, Pat. *Shout It From The Housetops*: Plainfield, NJ: Logos, 1972

Schillebeeckx, Edward. *Ministry*: New York, N.Y: Crossland, 1981

Bibles
The New American Bible: Cleveland, Ohio: Collins World, 1970

New International Version Bible: Grand Rapids, MI: Zondervan Publishing, 1973

The Holy Bible, Douay Version: New York, N.Y: P.J. Kennedy, 1914

The Jerusalem Bible: Garden City, N.Y: Doubleday & Co, 1966

Scriptural Reference Works

Clov, William. *Bible Readers Encyclopedia & Concordance*: London, Collins, 1977

Laymon, Charles M. *The Interpreter's One Volume Commentary On The Bible*: Nashville, TN: Abington Press, 1971

Packer, J. I. & Tenny, Merrill C. & White, Jr, Wm. *The Bible Almanac*: Nashville, TN: Thomas Nelson, 198

CPSIA information can be obtained at www.ICGtesting.com
Printed in the USA
BVOW081405121112

305324BV00001B/41/P